Bearded Dragon Care

Bearded Dragon Pet Owner's Guide.

Bearded Dragons care, behavior, diet, interacting, costs and health.

By

Ben Team

D1602752

Published by: IMB Publishing

Table of Contents

Foreword

Of all the reptiles commonly kept as pets, few are as well-suited for captivity as Pogona Vitticeps or inland bearded dragons are.

They reach impressive, yet not unmanageable sizes; they generally possess docile, unimposing temperaments; and, perhaps most importantly, bearded dragons are hardy creatures who thrive under relatively simple husbandry regimens.

Additionally, because bearded dragons – like all Australian natives – may not be exported under normal circumstances, the vast majority of those in European and North American markets are the result of captive breeding programs. This means that keepers can sidestep many of the challenges associated with wild-caught animals, such as parasites.

***

Despite the numerous characteristics that make bearded dragons excel in captivity, they possess a few characteristics that present challenges to keepers.

For example, bearded dragons are heliothermic ("sun-loving") lizards, who have very specific heating and lighting requirements. If they are to thrive, the keeper must address these issues adequately.

Additionally, bearded dragons are omnivores, who not only require live insect food, they also need access to nutritious fruits and vegetables if they are to remain healthy and develop properly. Caring for the insects and ensuring that they receive a wide variety of vegetable-based foods is often challenging for beginning keepers.

Additionally, because bearded dragons are voracious eaters, they produce a significant quantity of waste. Accordingly, their enclosures require daily cleaning. Failing to keep their habitats adequately clean can result in a variety of health problems, from infections to parasite infestations.

***

Ultimately, bearded dragons are rewarding pets, but they also present a number of challenges.

If you are ready to meet these challenges, learn all you can about your new pet and strive to ensure your lizard maintains a high-quality of life, then a bearded dragon may be the perfect pet reptile for you.

About the Author

Ben Team is an environmental educator and author with over 16 years of professional reptile-keeping experience.

Ben currently maintains www.FootstepsInTheForest.com, where he shares information, narration and observations of the natural world. When not writing about plants, animals and habitats, Ben enjoys spending time with his beautiful wife.

PART I: THE BEARDED DRAGON

Properly caring for any animal requires an understanding of the species and its place in the natural world. This includes digesting subjects as disparate as anatomy and ecology, diet and geography, and reproduction and physiology.

It is only by learning what your pet is, how it lives, what it does that you can achieve the primary goal of animal husbandry: Providing your pet with the highest quality of life possible.

Chapter 1: Bearded Dragon Description and Anatomy

In terms of basic body plan, Pogona Vitticeps or inland bearded dragons resemble most of their close relatives – a group of lizards known as agamas. They have stocky bodies, large heads, long tails and a sprawling body posture. However, despite these similarities, bearded dragons display several physical differences from their relatives, making it easy to distinguish them from other agamids.

Size

Bearded dragons hatch from their eggs measuring approximately 3 to 4 inches (7 to 10 centimeters) in total length, and weighing about 0.1 ounce (2 to 3 grams). With access to an adequate quantity and quality of food, bearded dragons grow quickly and reach maturity within their first year of life. Most adults are about 18 inches (45 centimeters) in length, but they vary in size from about 16 to 24 inches (40 to 60 centimeters). Adults weigh about 0.5 to 1 pound (225 to 450 grams), although particularly large specimens may weight slightly more than this.

Color and Pattern

In the wild, bearded dragons are primarily clad in brown and gray tones. Assorted white and black markings adorn various parts of the body, particularly down the center of the back. Often, this takes the form of a series of blotches that travel down the lizards' backs, with a pair of light-colored stripes occurring on both sides of the blotches.

These are two very colorful bearded dragons.

Small areas of light color – most commonly yellow or orange – may adorn the spikes on the side of the body or small washes can be present near the eyes or distributed throughout the beard.

However, captive bearded dragons have been selectively bred for attractive color (as well as hardiness and temperament) for many generations. This means that most captive bred bearded dragons display significant amounts of red, orange, yellow, white or purple mixed with their base colors (brown and gray).

Especially attractive individuals may be primarily clad in oranges, reds or whites; or they may possess a rainbow of colors.

Most young bearded dragons display only a hint of their future color potential, and the intensity and extent of the desired colors often increases with age.

All bearded dragons, regardless of the particular colors they possess, are capable of some degree of color change. This primarily occurs along a dark-light spectrum, but their pattern elements can become more or less conspicuous as well. Additionally, many bearded dragons adopt darker beard colors during the spring and summer.

Body

Bearded dragons have squat, rounded bodies. They are covered in a variety of different scale types; some are relatively flat, while others come to a sharp point. These scales and spines help to make bearded dragons look more formidable to predators, but most of the spikes yield under gentle pressure, making them an empty threat.

A close up of the spines located on a bearded dragon's torso.

11

Bearded dragons will flatten their bodies when drinking water, basking in the sunshine or attempting to dissuade predators.

Head

The heads of bearded dragons are very large and triangular in shape. Although most of the head is protected by a litany of sharp, keeled scales and spines, the largest spines typically lie along the back of the head and behind the mouth and jaw. The throat area is covered in numerous small scales. When frightened, irritated or interacting with other bearded dragons, the lizard may "puff out" these scales. This increases the apparent size of the lizards, which may dissuade predators or intimidate rivals.

Eyes

Bearded dragons have large eyes, located prominently on each side of the head. A small ridge lies above each, which partially shades the eye from the sun and offers some protection from injury.

The eyes of bearded dragons feature muscular eyelids, which can open and close at will. The edges of the eyelids possess small, eyelash-like scales. The skin around the eyes often bears bold colors (yellow and orange being the most common), but the irises are typically brown to yellow in color.

Bearded dragons also possess primitive organ, resembling a discolored scale on the tops of their heads. Called the parietal eye, the organ collects light and relays the information to the lizard's pineal gland. Despite being called an "eye," this organ cannot resolve images as typical eyes can.

Ears

Unlike some other lizards, bearded dragons have obvious ears. The triangular tympanum (ear drum) is clearly visible on the rear portion of the side of the lizard's head. The entire ear is set into a concave portion of the lizard's head, which helps to provide some protection to the ear.

Nostrils

Bearded dragon nostrils are conspicuous, triangular-shaped openings, located on either side of the animal's snout. They are surrounded by an unbroken, scaly ring, which may or may not be the same color as the surrounding scales.

Mouth and Teeth

Bearded dragons have large, spacious mouths which enable them to consume relatively bulky prey items. Like most other lizards, they lack a secondary palate.

Bearded dragons (like most other agamid lizards) have acrodont, rather than pleurodont dentition. This means that their small triangular teeth attach to the upper surface of the jaw bones. These teeth are primarily used for shredding vegetation.

Acrodont teeth are rarely replaced if lost, so most bearded dragons will keep their teeth throughout their lives. However, the nature of the way the teeth are connected to the jaw bone predisposes bearded dragons to periodontal disease.

Limbs and Feet

Like most other tetrapods, bearded dragons have four muscular legs which lie along the sides of the lizard's body. Their legs are capable of supporting their bodies above the ground, but during periods of rest, they are held out to the sides of the body.

Five toes adorn each of their four feet. Bearded dragons have long, curved nails, which extend from the tip of each toe. These nails help them to grip the substrate and climb tree branches and other rough objects.

Vent

The vent is a transverse opening located under the base of a bearded dragon's tail, slightly behind the rear legs. This forms the exit point for all reproductive structures and products (eggs), as well as the end products of the digestive and renal systems.

The vent usually remains closed, and opens slightly when the lizards defecate, release urates, copulate or deposit eggs.

Tail

Bearded dragons have long, cylindrical tails. The animals have some degree of control of the muscles of the tail base, but they cannot grip items with the tip of the tail. Instead, the tip of the tail simply follows behind them. Sometimes they hold the tip of the tail above the ground, at other times they allow it to drag.

Many bearded dragons – especially captives that have been raised in communal cages – have nipped tail tips. As long as the damage caused by the wound (usually inflicted by a conspecific cagemate) is not extensive, damaged tails rarely have serious effects on the dragon's quality of life.

Bearded dragons do not voluntarily jettison their tails, as some lizards do. Bearded dragons who lose their tails (in whole or in part) are not capable of regenerating them.

Internal Organs

The internal anatomy of bearded dragons differs relatively little from that of other lizards or tetrapods in general.

Bearded dragons draw oxygen in through their nostrils; pipe it through the trachea and into the lungs. Here, blood exchanges carbon dioxide for oxygen, before it is pumped to the various body parts via the heart and blood vessels.

While the bearded dragon's heart features only three true chambers (two atria and a single ventricle), a septum keeps the ventricle divided at most times, allowing the heart to operate similarly to a four-chambered, mammalian heart. This means that in practice, bearded dragons keep their oxygenated and deoxygenated blood relatively separate in the heart.

Their digestive system is comprised of an esophagus, stomach, small intestine, large intestine and a terminal chamber called the cloaca. The stomach has some ability to stretch to accommodate food.

The liver resides near the center of the animal's torso, with the gall bladder sitting directly behind it. While the gall bladder stores bile, the liver provides a number of functions relating to digestion, metabolism and filtration. Kidneys, which lie almost directly behind the lungs, filter wastes from the lizard's bloodstream.

Like other lizards, bearded dragons control their bodies via their brain and nervous system. Their endocrine and exocrine glands work much as they do in other vertebrates.

Reproductive Organs

Like all squamates, male bearded dragons have paired reproductive organs, called hemipenes. When not in use, males keep their hemipenes inside the bases of their tails. When they attempt to mate with a female, they evert one of the hemipenes and insert it into the female's cloaca.

The paired nature of the male sex organs ensures that males can continue to breed if they suffer injury to one of the hemipenes. This paired arrangement also allows male bearded dragons to mate with females on either side of their body.

Females have paired ovaries, which produce ova (eggs), and they have paired oviducts, which store the eggs after they are released from the ovaries. The eggs are shelled and held inside the oviducts until it is time to deposit the eggs. At this time, the eggs are passed from the oviducts into the cloaca and out of the body via the vent.

Chapter 2: Bearded Dragon Biology and Behavior

Bearded dragons exhibit a number of biological and behavioral adaptations that allow them to survive in their natural habitats.

Shedding

Like other scaled reptiles, dragons shed their old skin to reveal new, fresh skin underneath. Bearded dragons do not shed their skin in one piece, as most snakes do. Instead, bearded dragons tend to shed in several separate pieces over the course of a day or two.

Bearded dragons may consume their shed skin, but this is not as common a phenomenon as it is in some other lizards, such as geckos.

Metabolism and Digestion

Bearded dragons are ectothermic ("cold-blooded") animals, whose internal metabolism depends on their body temperature. When warm, their bodily functions proceed more rapidly; when cold, their bodily functions proceed slowly.

This also means that the lizards digest more effectively at suitably warm temperatures than they do at suboptimal temperatures. Their appetites also vary with temperature, and if the temperatures drop below the preferred range, they may cease feeding entirely.

A bearded dragon's body temperature largely follows ambient air temperatures, but they also absorb and reflect radiant heat, such as that coming from the sun. The lizards try to keep their body temperature within the preferred range by employing behaviors that allow them adjust their temperature.

For example, bearded dragons bask to raise their temperature when they are too cool. This typically involves orienting their body so that they are perpendicular with the sun's rays. Additionally, some individuals may exhibit darker colors when basking or flatten their bodies to help absorb more infrared rays.

By contrast, when it is necessary to cool off, dragons may move into the shade or gape their mouths to release excess heat.

Growth Rate and Lifespan

Bearded dragons grow quickly, often doubling their size each month during their first few months of life. By the time the lizards reach about 12 inches (30 centimeters) in length, their growth rate slows considerably.

However, there is a great deal of variation in individual growth rates, and invariably some clutch mates grow much more quickly or slowly than their siblings do. This can lead some lizards to be twice the size of their siblings within a few months' time.

Most bearded dragons should reach their adult size within their first year of life, although adults may continue to grow (albeit more slowly) during their second year of life.

Bearded dragons probably exhibit a high turnover rate in the wild. The majority of the hatchlings likely end up as prey for small predators, but those that reach maturity are likely to live for 3 to 5 years or so.

Bearded dragons climb higher off the ground as temperatures increase.

However, in captivity, where the lizards are provided with unlimited food, veterinary care and protection from parasites and predators, bearded dragons often live much longer than this.

The average lifespan of a captive bearded dragon is between about 5 and 10 years. However, there is at least one report of a bearded dragon living for more than 19 years. (Müller, 2014)

Foraging Behavior

Bearded dragons forage actively for food and they ambush passing insects when the opportunity arises. Bearded dragons primarily rely on their vision to locate prey and edible plants, but they may taste potential food items (particularly plant-based foods) with their fleshy tongue before consuming them as well. (William E Cooper, 2000)

Bearded dragons spend a lot of time in the wild resting on elevated perches. Those who spot potential prey items scurrying by may descend and travel several feet to capture it.

Diel and Seasonal Activity

Bearded dragons are almost entirely diurnal animals, who spend their days basking in the sun, foraging for food, seeking mates and defending themselves from predators.

With the onset of night, most bearded dragons find a safe place to sleep until dawn. This may take the form of an exposed perch, but most individuals find a rock crevice or patch of dense vegetation in which they remain throughout the night.

Bearded dragons are most active during the Australian spring, summer and fall. They typically remain inactive during the bulk of the winter. Nevertheless, individuals may emerge from their burrows and bask during unusually warm days.

Defensive Strategies and Tactics

Crypsis is the first method by which bearded dragons seek to defend themselves. The combination of their camouflaged colors, flattened body, sedentary behavior and numerous skin projections makes them blend in quite well in their natural habitats.

When crypsis fails, bearded dragons may elect to flee, but as they lack the high-end speed of many other lizards, bearded dragons may instead stand their grown. When doing so, the lizards will usually turn and face their adversary, while simultaneously displaying several distinct defensive behaviors.

Bearded dragons typically expand their throat and gape their mouths during these displays, which makes them look larger and more intimidating. Their beard color may darken slightly during these displays and the sharp scales on the throat region stand up, causing them to look prickly. Bearded dragons may also expand their body cavity during this time.

If these measures fail to repel the predator, the lizard may ultimately resort to biting. While their teeth are relatively small, large bearded dragons can inflict a rather strong pinch with their jaws. The bites from small bearded dragons are harmless, and unlikely to deter most predators.

This bearded dragon is displaying threat posture.

Reproduction

Bearded dragons are prolific breeders, who produce a large number of small offspring. Breeding can take place during any portion of the active season, but is most common during the spring and early summer. Males usually maintain and defend a small territory from other males.

Males will usually attempt to breed with any females that pass through their territory. But because females do not always acquiesce to such advances, these encounters often appear violent. Males may repeatedly bite the females to hold them in place.

Over the course of a breeding season, males may mate with several females. Females may mate with more than one male, but they can retain the sperm from a single mating and deposit multiple clutches of eggs over the course of the breeding season.

Females deposit eggs about 3 to 5 weeks after successful mating. As the time for egg deposition nears, the females excavate a small egg chamber in the soil, often at the base of a tree, shrub or rock. Once completed, the female will turn around and deposit between 10 and 30 eggs.

The female will cover the egg chamber upon completing parturition. Once she leaves, she will have no further contact with the young. Bearded dragons provide no care for the hatchlings, and may even predate upon them.

The young begin hatching from their eggs about 40 to 85 days to hatch, depending upon the temperatures in the egg chamber. They may remain in their shells for a day or two, but soon, they will dig their way out of the soil.

Chapter 3: Classification and Taxonomy

Scientists currently recognize the inland bearded dragon* as *Pogona vitticeps*. Like all other living species, bearded dragons are placed within a hierarchical classification scheme.

Kingdom: Animalia

Phylum: Chordata

Class: Reptilia

Order: Squamata

Family: Agamidae

Genus: *Pogona*

Species: *vitticeps*

The genus *Pogona* contains 7 different species (including the inland bearded dragon). These represent some of the closest living relatives of bearded dragons – including the dwarf bearded dragon (*Pogona minor*), the eastern bearded dragon (*Pogona barbata*) and the western bearded dragon (*Pogona minima*).

Bearded dragons are currently recognized as a single species with no described subspecies.

*Although hobbyists normally refer to these lizards as bearded dragons, a better common name is *inland* bearded dragon. This helps to distinguish the species from its close relatives without resorting to zoological nomenclature.

Chapter 4: The Bearded Dragon's World

To maintain a bearded dragon successfully, you must understand the animal's native habitat and provide a reasonable facsimile of it.

Range

Bearded dragons inhabit a large swath of central Australia. They can be found living in the southeastern portion of the Northern Territory, southwest Queensland, western New South Wales, northern Victoria, and most of South Australia.

Several congeneric relatives also live in Australia. In fact, the only portions of the continent that lack some representative of the genus are the northern reaches of the Northern Territory and Queensland.

Climate

The climate of central Australia varies slightly along the north-south axis of their range. The climate in the northern reaches of their range is tropical, but it shifts to sub-tropical and eventually temperate in the southern reaches of their range.

Rainfall levels are very low in the interior of the continent, typically measuring less than 10 inches (25 centimeters) per year.

Habitat

Several different habitat types lie within the range of bearded dragons, but grasslands, deserts and other arid areas dominate the region.

Bearded dragons typically inhabit areas with some nearby vegetation – they are not common in sand-dune dominated locations.

Natural Diet

Recent studies (Leeuwen, 2015) have confirmed what bearded dragon enthusiasts have long thought: Bearded dragons are opportunistic predators, who consume a wide variety of arthropods and supplement their diet with leafy green vegetation.

The specific prey species consumed by bearded dragons likely varies from one location to the next, as well as from one season to the next. Termites are important during their mass emergences, but beetles, grasshoppers, locusts, crickets and flies are also frequently consumed items.

Natural Predators

A variety of large and medium-sized predators likely prey upon bearded dragons, although specific studies are lacking. Some of the animals that presumably prey on bearded dragons include:

- Other lizards, particularly goannas (*Varanus* spp.)
- Birds of prey
- Large snakes, especially pythons
- Dingoes
- Domestic dogs and cats

Status in the Wild

While they have not been formally assessed by the IUCN Redlist of Threatened Species, bearded dragons are generally considered to be plentiful in the wild.

PART II: BEARDED DRAGON HUSBANDRY

Once equipped with a basic understanding of what bearded dragons *are* (Chapter 1 and Chapter 3), where they *live* (Chapter 4), and what they *do* (Chapter 2) you can begin learning about their captive care.

Animal husbandry is an evolving pursuit. Keepers shift their strategies frequently as they incorporate new information and ideas into their husbandry paradigms.

There are few "right" or "wrong" answers, and what works in one situation may not work in another. Accordingly, you may find that different authorities present different, and sometimes conflicting, information regarding the care of these dragons.

In all cases, you must strive to learn as much as you can about your pet and its natural habitat, so that you may provide it with the best quality of life possible.

Chapter 5: Bearded Dragons as Pets

Bearded dragons can make rewarding pets, but you must know what to expect before adding one to your home and family. This includes not only understanding the nature of the care they require, but also the costs associated with this care.

Assuming that you feel confident in your ability to care for a bearded dragon and endure the associated financial burdens, you can begin seeking your individual pet.

Understanding the Commitment

Keeping a bearded dragon as a pet requires a substantial commitment. You will be responsible for your pet's well-being for the rest of its life. Although bearded dragons are not particularly long-lived animals, their lifespans are not trivial.

Can you be sure that you will still want to care for your pet several years in the future? Do you know what your living situation will be? What changes will have occurred in your family? How will your working life have changed over this time?

You must consider all of these possibilities before acquiring a new pet. Failing to do so often leads to apathy, neglect and even resentment, which is not good for you or your pet lizard.

Neglecting your pet is wrong, and in some locations, a criminal offense. You must continue to provide quality care for your dragon, even once the novelty has worn off, and it is no longer fun to clean the cage and purchase crickets a few times a week.

Once you purchase a lizard, its well-being becomes your responsibility until it passes away at the end of a long life, or you have found someone who will agree to adopt the animal for you.

Unfortunately, this is rarely an easy task. You may begin with thoughts of selling your pet to help recoup a small part of your investment, but these efforts will largely fall flat.

While professional breeders may profit from the sale of bearded dragons, amateurs are at a decided disadvantage. Only a tiny sliver of the general population is interested in reptilian pets, and only a small subset of these are interested in keeping bearded dragons.

Of those who are interested in acquiring a bearded dragon, most would rather start fresh, by *purchasing* a small hatchling or juvenile from an established breeder, rather than adopting your questionable animal *for free*.

After having difficulty finding a willing party to purchase or adopt your animal, many owners try to donate their pet to a local zoo. Unfortunately, this rarely works either.

Zoos are not interested in your pet lizard, no matter how pretty he is and how readily he snatches crickets from your fingers. He is a pet with little to no reliable provenance and questionable health status. This is simply not the type of animal zoos are eager to add to their multi-million dollar collections.

Zoos obtain most of their animals from other zoos and museums; failing that, they obtain their animals directly from their land of origin. As a rule, they do not accept donated pets.

No matter how difficult it becomes to find a new home for your unwanted dragon, you must never release non-native reptiles into the wild.

Bearded dragons can colonize places outside their native range (and they already have done so in some places). While these exotic populations do not appear to be causing serious ecological problems yet, further research is necessary before the potential for serious ecological damage can be ruled out.

Additionally, released or escaped reptiles cause a great deal of distress to those who are frightened by them. This leads local municipalities to adopt pet restrictions or ban reptile keeping entirely.

While the chances of an escaped or released dragon harming anyone are very low, it is unlikely that those who fear reptiles will see the threat as minor.

The Costs of Captivity
Reptiles are often marketed as low-cost pets. While true in a relative sense (the costs associated with dog, cat, horse or tropical fish husbandry are often much higher than they are for bearded dragons), potential keepers must still prepare for the financial implications of dragon ownership.

At the outset, you must budget for the acquisition of your pet, as well as the costs of purchasing or constructing a habitat. Unfortunately, while many keepers plan for these costs, they typically fail to consider the on-going costs, which will quickly eclipse the initial startup costs.

Startup Costs

One surprising fact most new keepers learn is the enclosure and equipment will often cost more than the animal does (except in the case of very high-priced specimens).

Prices fluctuate from one market to the next, but in general, the least you will spend on a male (females are often slightly less expensive) bearded dragon is about $200 (£135), while the least you will spend on the *initial* habitat and assorted equipment will be about $250 (£170). Replacement equipment and food will represent additional (and ongoing) expenses.

Examine the charts on the following pages to get an idea of three different pricing scenarios. While the specific prices listed will vary based on innumerable factors, the charts are instructive for first-time buyers.

The first scenario details a budget-minded keeper, trying to spend as little as possible. The second example estimates the costs for a keeper with a moderate budget, and the third example provides a case study for extravagant shoppers, who want an expensive dragon and top-notch equipment.

These charts are only provided estimates; your experience may vary based on a variety of factors.

Inexpensive Option

Hatchling Bearded Dragon	$50 (£34)
Plastic Storage Tub	$25 (£17)
Heat Lamp Fixture and Bulbs	$20 (£13)
Full Spectrum Fixture and Bulbs	$50 (£34)
Substrate, Perches, etc.	$50 (£34)
Infrared Thermometer	$35 (£24)
Digital Indoor-Outdoor Thermometer	$20 (£13)
Food Dish, Forceps, Spray Bottles, Misc.	$25 (£17)
Total	$275 (£186)

Moderate Option

Premium Bearded Dragon Hatchling	$200 (£140)
Homemade Habitat	$100 (£68)
Heat Lamp Fixture and Bulbs	$20 (£13)
Full Spectrum Fixture and Bulbs	$50 (£34)
Substrate, Perches, etc.	$50 (£34)
Infrared Thermometer	$35 (£24)
Digital Indoor-Outdoor Thermometer	$20 (£13)
Food Dish, Forceps, Spray Bottles, Misc.	$25 (£17)
Total	$500 (£348)

Premium Option

Premium Bearded Dragon Juvenile	$300 (£208)
Premium Commercial Enclosure	$500 (£340)
Heat Lamp and Bulbs	$20 (£13)
Full Spectrum Fixture and Bulbs	$50 (£34)
Substrate, Perches, etc.	$50 (£34)
Infrared Thermometer	$35 (£24)
Digital Indoor-Outdoor Thermometer	$20 (£13)
Food Dish, Forceps, Spray Bottles, Misc.	$25 (£17)
Total	$1000 (£697)

Ongoing Costs

The ongoing costs of bearded dragon ownership primarily fall into one of three categories: food, maintenance and veterinary care.

Food costs are the most significant of the three, but they are relatively consistent and somewhat predictable. Some maintenance costs are easy to calculate, but things like equipment malfunctions are impossible to predict with any certainty. Veterinary expenses are hard to predict and vary wildly from one year to the next.

Food Costs

Food is the single greatest ongoing cost you will experience while caring for your dragon. To obtain a reasonable estimate of your yearly food costs, you must consider the number of meals you will feed your pet per year and the cost of each meal.

The amount of food your dragon consumes will vary based on numerous factors, including his size, the average temperatures in his habitat, his health and the size of the food items. However, a reasonable estimate would be in the ballpark of 10 items per feeding. If you feed your pet seven times per week, he will require 70 insects per week, or about 3500 per year.

Most common feeder insects cost between $0.01 and $0.10 cents each, depending on the species and size. Most commercially produced insects are cheaper when purchased in bulk.

Accordingly, it will cost you somewhere between $35 and $350 per year (£24 to £245) to feed your pet. This estimate spans an order of magnitude, but it remains somewhat helpful for planning your costs (it also speaks to the importance of minimizing food costs and waste).

Professional breeders utilizing efficient feeding systems and bulk purchasing power incur costs at the lower end of that range, while pet owners who purchase their insects at retail prices and fail to use them efficiently will undoubtedly find themselves at the high end of this range.

Your bearded dragon also requires vegetable-based foods, which represent additional costs. Even if you only spend $2.00 per week on vegetables, that amounts to over $100 (£68) each year.

One of the best ways to sidestep these costs is to grow your own vegetables for your dragon, but this often requires space (and suitable climate) which is not always available.

Veterinary Costs

Unlike many other pet reptiles, who probably benefit from an annual veterinary exam, bearded dragons do not tolerate stress well, and any non-essential travel should be avoided.

While you should always seek veterinary advice at the first sign of illness, it is probably not wise to haul your healthy dragon to the vet's office for no reason. Accordingly, you shouldn't incur any veterinary expenses unless your pet falls ill.

However, veterinary care can become very expensive, very quickly. In addition to a basic exam or phone consultation, your lizard may need cultures, x-rays or other diagnostic tests performed. In light of this, wise keepers budget at least $200 to $300 (£136 to £204) each year to cover any emergency veterinary costs.

Maintenance Costs
It is important to plan for both routine and unexpected maintenance costs. Commonly used items, such as paper towels, disinfectant and top soil are rather easy to calculate. However, it is not easy to know how many burned out light bulbs, cracked misting units or faulty thermostats you will have to replace in a given year.

Those who keep their dragons in simple enclosures will find that about $50 (£34) covers their yearly maintenance costs. By contrast, those who maintain elaborate habitats may spend $200 (£136) or more each year.

Always try to purchase frequently used supplies, such as light bulbs, paper towels and disinfectants in bulk to maximize your savings. It is often beneficial to consult with local reptile-keeping clubs, who often pool their resources to attain greater buying power.

Myths and Misunderstandings

Myth: Bearded dragons need "friends" or they will get lonely.

Fact: While a handful of dragon species appear to thrive in small groups, bearded dragons are solitary animals that spend the bulk of their lives alone. Communally caged bearded dragons are likely to become stressed; males may engage in violent conflicts with other males or stress females with incessant breeding attempts.

Young bearded dragons often cohabitate well with each other, as long as their habitats are suitably large and feature numerous visual barriers. However, just because they will tolerate being raised in groups does not mean they enjoy it – they would much rather be in their own cage.

It is also important to point out that even dragons that appear to be cohabitating peacefully are usually suffering from the effects of chronic stress. Their keepers simply fail to observe the subtle signs exhibited by the lizards.

Myth: Reptiles grow in proportion to the size of their cage and then stop.

Fact: Reptiles do no such thing. Most healthy lizards, snakes and turtles grow throughout their lives, although the rate of growth slows with age (a very few stop growing with maturity, although this is not influenced by the size of their cage).

Placing them in a small cage in an attempt to stunt their growth is an unthinkably cruel practice, which is more likely to sicken or kill your pet than stunt its growth.

Providing a bearded dragon with an inadequately spacious cage is a sure recipe for illness, maladaptation and eventual death.

Myth: Bearded dragons can subsist entirely on prepared, commercial diets.

Fact: While commercial bearded dragon diets may make a suitable component of your pet's diet, they shouldn't form the bulk of it. Instead, you should primarily feed your lizard a variety of insects and leafy green vegetables, with small bits of commercial food added periodically, if you wish.

Myth: Reptiles have no emotions and do not suffer.

Fact: While dragons have very primitive brains and do not have emotions comparable to those of higher mammals, they can absolutely suffer.

Always treat reptiles with the same compassion you would offer a dog, cat or horse.

Myth: Bearded dragons are tame lizards that never bite.

Fact: While bearded dragons are typically calm, docile animals that are not inclined to bite, there are no guarantees that they will not do so. Stressed or frightened bearded dragons may bite if they feel that escape is impossible.

Bearded dragons possess teeth, although they are relatively short and unlikely to cause deep wounds.

Acquiring Your Bearded Dragon

Modern reptile enthusiasts can acquire bearded dragons from a variety of sources, each with a different set of pros and cons.

Pet stores are one of the first places many people see bearded dragons, and they become the de facto source of pets for many beginning keepers. While they do offer some unique benefits to prospective keepers, pet stores are not always the best place to purchase a dragon; so, consider all of the available options, including breeders and reptile swap meets, before making a purchase.

Pet Stores

Pet stores offer a number of benefits to keepers shopping for bearded dragons, including convenience: They usually stock all of the equipment your new lizard needs, including cages, heating devices and food items.

Additionally, they offer you the chance to inspect the lizard up close before purchase. In some cases, you may be able to choose from more than one specimen. Many pet stores provide health guarantees for a short period, that provides some recourse if your new pet turns out to be ill.

However, pet stores are not always the ideal place to purchase your new pet. Pet stores are retail establishments, and as such, you will usually pay more for your new pet than you would from a breeder.

Additionally, pet stores rarely know the pedigree of the animals they sell, and they will rarely know the lizard's date of birth, or other pertinent information. Only a handful of pet stores will be able to distinguish among the various locales of bearded dragon, so specimens may also be mislabeled.

Other drawbacks associated with pet stores primarily relate to the staff's inexperience. While some pet stores concentrate on reptiles and may educate their staff about proper dragon care, many others are provide incorrect advice to their customers.

It is also worth considering the increased exposure to pathogens that pet store animals endure, given the constant flow of animals through such facilities.

Reptile Expos

Reptile expos offer another option for purchasing a bearded dragon. Reptile expos often feature resellers, breeders and retailers in the same room, all selling various types of dragons and other reptiles.

Often, the prices at such events are quite reasonable and you are often able to select from many different lizards. However, if you have a problem, it may be difficult to find the seller after the event is over.

Breeders

Because they usually offer unparalleled information and support to their customers, breeders are generally the best place for most novices to shop for bearded dragons. Additionally, breeders often know the species well, and are better able to help you learn the husbandry techniques necessary for success.

For those seeking a particular type of bearded dragon, breeders are often the only option. This is especially true for those seeking dragons from underrepresented locations. The same principle holds true for those seeking spectacular individuals from proven bloodlines – the only place to purchase such dragons are from breeders.

The primary disadvantage of buying from a breeder is that you must often make such purchases from a distance, either by phone or via the internet. Nevertheless, most established breeders are happy to provide you with photographs of the animal you will be purchasing, as well as his or her parents.

Selecting Your Bearded Dragon

Not all dragons are created equally, so it is important to select a healthy individual that will give you the best chance of success.

Practically speaking, the most important criterion to consider is the health of the animal. However, the sex, age and history of the lizard are also important things to consider.

Health Checklist

Always check your dragon thoroughly for signs of injury or illness before purchasing it. If you are purchasing the animal from someone in a different part of the country, you must inspect it immediately upon delivery. Notify the seller promptly if the animal exhibits any health problems.

Avoid the temptation to acquire or accept a sick or injured animal in hopes of nursing him back to health. Not only are you likely to incur substantial veterinary costs while treating your new pet, you will likely fail in your attempts to restore the lizard to full health. Sick dragons rarely recover in the hands of novices (or, for that matter, experts).

Additionally, by purchasing injured or diseased animals, you incentivize poor husbandry on the part of the retailer. If retailers lose money on sick or injured animals, they will take steps to avoid this eventuality, by acquiring healthier stock in the first place, and providing better care for their charges.

As much as is possible, try to observe the following features:

- **Observe the lizard's skin**. It should be free of lacerations and other damage. Pay special attention to those areas that frequently sustain damage, such as the tip of the lizard's tail, the toes and the tip of the snout. A small cut or abrasion may be relatively easy to treat, but significant abrasions and cuts are likely to become infected and require significant treatment.

- **Gently check the lizard's crevices and creases for mites and ticks**. Mites are about the size of a flake of pepper, and they may be black, brown or red. Mites often move about on the lizard, whereas ticks – if attached and feeding – do not move. Avoid purchasing any animal that has either parasite. Additionally, you should avoid purchasing any other animals from this source, as they are likely to harbor parasites as well.

- **Examine the lizard's eyes, ears and nostrils**. The eyes should not be sunken, and they should be free of discharge. The nostrils should be clear and dry – lizards with runny noses or those who blow bubbles are likely to be suffering from a respiratory infection. However, be aware that lizards often get some water in their nostrils while drinking water. This is no cause for concern.

- **Gently palpate the animal and ensure no lumps or anomalies are apparent**. Lumps in the muscles or abdominal cavity may indicate parasites, abscesses or tumors.

- **Observe the lizard's demeanor**. Healthy lizards are aware of their environment and react to stimuli. When active, the lizard should calmly explore his environment. While you may wish to avoid purchasing an aggressive, defensive or flighty animal, these behaviors do not necessarily indicate a health problem.

- **Check the lizard's vent**. The vent should be clean and free of smeared feces. Smeared feces can indicate parasites or bacterial infections.

- **Check the lizard's appetite**. If possible, ask the retailer to feed the lizard a cricket, super worm or roach. A healthy dragon should usually exhibit a strong food drive, although failing to eat is not *necessarily* a bad sign – the lizard may not be hungry.

The Age

Hatchling bearded dragons are very fragile until they reach about one month of age. Before this, they are unlikely to thrive in the hands of beginning keepers.

Accordingly, most beginners should purchase two- or three-month-old juveniles, who have already become well established. Animals of this age tolerate the changes associated with a new home better than very young specimens do. Further, given their greater size, they will better tolerate temperature and humidity extremes than smaller animals will.

Mature animals are rarely preferable to juveniles, as they may have become accustomed to their surroundings and fail to adapt to their new home. Experienced keepers can often navigate such a transition, but beginners are better served by purchasing a younger animal.

The Sex

Unless you are attempting to breed bearded dragons, you should select a male pet. Females are more likely to suffer from reproduction-related health problems than males, and they may deposit eggs whether you want them or not (of course, these eggs will be infertile if your lizard lives in isolation).

Males reach slightly larger sizes, although the difference is minor and has few husbandry implications.

Quarantine

Because new animals may have illnesses or parasites that could infect the rest of your collection, it is wise to quarantine all new acquisitions. This means that you should keep any new animal as separated from the rest of your pets as possible. Only once you have ensured that the new animal is healthy should you introduce it to the rest of your collection.

During the quarantine period, you should keep the new lizard in a simplified habitat, with a paper substrate, water bowl, basking spot and a few hiding places. Keep the temperature and humidity at ideal levels.

It is wise to obtain fecal samples from your lizard during the quarantine period. You can take these samples to your veterinarian, who can check them for signs of internal parasites. Always treat any existing parasite infestations before removing the animal from quarantine.

Always tend to quarantined animals last, as this reduces the chances of transmitting pathogens to your healthy animals. Do not wash quarantined water bowls or cage furniture with those belonging to your healthy animals. Whenever possible, use completely separate tools for quarantined animals and those that have been in your collection for some time.

Always be sure to wash your hands thoroughly after handling quarantined animals, their cages or their tools. Particularly careful keepers wear a smock or alternative clothing when handling quarantined animals.

Quarantine new acquisitions for a minimum of 30 days; 60 or 90 days is even better. Many zoos and professional breeders maintain 180- or 360-day-long quarantine periods.

Chapter 6: Providing the Captive Habitat

Providing your bearded dragon with appropriate housing is and essential aspect of captive care. In essence, the habitat you provide to your pet becomes his world.

In most respects, providing bearded dragons with a suitable captive habitat entails *functionally* replicating the various aspects of their wild habitats. In other words, the habitat needn't *look* like an arid Australian scrubland, but it must *function* like one.

After providing your pet with an enclosure (this chapter), you will need to provide the animal with the correct thermal environment (Chapter 7), lighting (Chapter 8), substrate (Chapter 9) and cage furniture (Chapter 9).

Enclosure

In "the old days," those inclined to keep reptiles had few choices with regard to caging. The two primary options were to build a custom cage from scratch or construct a lid to use with a fish aquarium.

By contrast, modern hobbyists have a variety of options from which to choose. In addition to building custom cages or adapting aquaria, dozens of different cage styles are available – each with different pros and cons.

Aquariums

Aquariums are popular choices for many pet reptiles and they are available at virtually every pet store in the country. However, they present several challenges for bearded dragon maintenance and are not ideal for this purpose.

While many 10- and 20-gallon aquariums have footprints that are acceptable for housing very small bearded dragons, few aquariums are manufactured in the appropriate layout for adults. While small aquariums have a large footprint relative to their volume, large aquariums have small footprints relative to their volume. This is because they are designed for fish rather than reptiles, who use their available space in different ways.

Also, aquariums are built so that the top of the enclosure serves as the opening, rather than the front. This can make it difficult to access the animal or clean the enclosure if the heat lamps and full-spectrum bulbs are resting on top of the cage.

One final, but important, drawback to aquariums is their weight. Large aquariums – particularly those loaded with substrate, rocks and perches --

are very heavy. Most will require two people to lift and move. Additionally, the glass construction makes aquariums very fragile enclosures, which can break very easily

Commercial Cages
Commercially produced reptile enclosures (such as those designed for snakes) are widely regarded as the best choice for bearded dragon maintenance.

Most commercial cages are made from plastic or glass, and they feature doors on the front of the enclosure, rather than on the top. This means that they provide better access to the enclosure than aquariums do. Additionally, commercial reptile cages usually feature better footprint-to-volume ratios than aquariums do.

Commercial cages are usually sturdier than glass aquariums and lighter too. This makes them much easier to handle and move than aquariums.

Custom Built Cages
For keepers with access to tools and the desire and skill to use them, it is possible to construct homemade cages.

A number of materials are suitable for cage construction, and each has different pros and cons. Wood is commonly used, but must be adequately sealed to avoid rotting, warping or absorbing offensive odors.

Plastic sheeting is a very good material, but few have the necessary skills, knowledge and tools necessary for cage construction. Additionally, some plastics may have extended off-gassing times.

Glass can be used, whether glued to itself or when used with a frame. Custom-built glass cages can be better than aquariums, as you can design them in dimensions that are appropriate for bearded dragons. Additionally, they can be constructed in such a way that the door is on the front of the cage, rather than the top.

In all cases, the cages should be designed to contain the lizard safely, provide an adequate amount of floor space and allow the keeper suitable access.

Plastic Storage Containers
Plastic storage containers, such as those used for shoes, sweaters or food, can make sufficient enclosures for bearded dragons.

While they are not particularly pretty, plastic storage boxes offer a number of advantages over other cage styles. This is especially true when housing small lizards.

For example, plastic storage boxes are much lighter than either aquariums or commercial cages, and they are less likely to break. Plastic storage containers are almost always much cheaper than cages or aquariums of similar size.

Usually, in order for plastic storage containers to serve as convenient housing, they must be tall enough to contain the lizards without the need for a lid. Obviously, this is not advisable in homes with pets or small children.

Plastic containers are rarely available in sizes appropriate for large adult bearded dragons, but enterprising keepers may use cattle stock tanks or prefabricated pond liners instead.

Outdoor Enclosures
Outdoor enclosures are great for giving your bearded dragon access to natural sunlight. While most keepers will only be able to do so during the warmest portions of the year, those living in the American southwest can probably keep bearded dragons outdoors year-round.

To house your bearded dragon outdoors, you will need to erect a boundary of some type, constructed from either wood, stone, concrete or plastic planks. To keep the local predators from consuming your pets, you will need to place a screen or fence over the top of the enclosure.

Bury a short length of chain-link fencing or robust screen around the periphery of the enclosure to ensure digging predators cannot gain access to the cage.

You will need to place the enclosure in a place that receives adequate sunshine, so the lizards can bask and raise their body temperature effectively. However, the lizards must have access to shade, particularly during the middle of the day.

Dimensions
Dragons require a fair bit of space to thrive. Ideally, each adult bearded dragon should have about 8 to 10 square feet (0.75 to 1 square meter) of floor space in the enclosure. However, many keepers are successful providing less space than this. Minimally, each adult bearded dragon requires 6 square feet (0.5 square meter) of space.

Hatchlings and juveniles require less space than adults do. Bearded dragons between 4 and 8 inches in length are comfortable in about 1 to 2 square feet (0.1 to 0.2 square meters) of space. You can use an intermediate cage for lizards between 8 and 12 inches in length, with about 3 or 4 square feet (0.25 to 0.4 square meters) of space, but it is more economical to simply skip the intermediate cage and move lizards of this size into their adult, permanent enclosures.

While they do not require 6-foot-tall cages like some arboreal lizards do, bearded dragons appreciate some vertical space in their cage. In most cases, 18 to 24 inches (45 to 60 centimeters) of cage height is ideal.

Bearded dragons are essentially solitary lizards in the wild, but in captivity, they will often adjust to communal living arrangements. However, mature males should not be housed together, as they are likely to engage in brutal physical confrontations, which can leave them injured and stressed.

Chapter 7: Establishing the Thermal Environment

Providing the proper thermal environment is one of the most important aspects of reptile husbandry. As ectothermic ("cold blooded") animals, bearded dragons rely on the surrounding temperatures to regulate the rate at which their metabolism operates.

When afforded access to the appropriate temperatures, a bearded dragon's body can operate properly. By contrast,

Accordingly, the difference between a healthy, thriving lizard and one who spends a great deal of time at the veterinarian's office, battling infections and illness is access to the appropriate temperatures.

Providing your dragon with a suitable thermal environment requires you to understand your lizard's preferred body temperature, the right way to supply heat to the habitat and the correct way to monitor the temperatures inside the enclosure.

Preferred Body Temperature

While individuals may demonstrate slightly different preferences, bearded dragons generally prefer to maintain temperatures of about 91 degrees Fahrenheit (33 degrees Celsius) during the day. (SCHULTE, 2001) Although studies of the nocturnal body temperatures of wild dragons are lacking, inactive (sleeping) dragons allow their body temperatures to drop with the ambient air temperatures each night.

Thermoregulation Tactics

Bearded dragons are not completely helpless in the face of imperfect temperatures. They can usually remain active at ambient temperatures ranging from the low 60s to the high 90s (about 18 to 37 degrees Celsius).

When the ambient temperatures are outside of their preferred range, the lizards adjust their behavior to bring their body temperature back into the preferred range.

For example, on cool mornings, bearded dragons may flatten their bodies and display dark colors to help absorb as much solar radiation as possible. Conversely, they may attempt to cope with uncomfortably warm temperatures by retreating to the shade or gaping their mouths.

Additionally, studies of free-living bearded dragons show that the lizards tend to climb higher off the ground when temperatures rise. This exposes them to more air flow and puts distance between themselves and the hot ground below.

Thermal Gradients

To work in concert with the thermoregulatory behaviors of your pet, you must provide him or her with access to a variety of temperatures. In other words, you must supply your pet with a thermal gradient.

The best way to do this is by clustering the heating devices at one end of the habitat, thereby creating a basking spot (the warmest spot in the enclosure). The temperatures will slowly drop with increasing distance from the basking spot, which creates a *gradient* of *temperatures*.

Adjust the heating device until the ambient temperatures at the basking spot are about 91 to 95 degrees Fahrenheit (33 to 35 degrees Celsius) during the hottest part of the day. To maintain ambient air temperatures in this range at the basking spot, the surface temperatures at the basking spot will usually be higher than this. This is no cause for worry – surface temperatures on rocks or logs under the basking spot may reach 115 to 120 degrees Fahrenheit (46 to 49 degrees Celsius). As long as you can hold your hand on the surface indefinitely, it is unlikely to burn your lizard.

Because there is no heat source at the other end of the cage, the ambient temperature will gradually fall as your lizard moves away from the heat source. Ideally, the cool end of the cage should remain in the low 80s Fahrenheit (26 to 28 degrees Celsius) throughout the day.

Barriers, such as branches and vegetation, also help to create shaded patches, which provide additional thermal options for your pet. This mimics the way temperatures vary from one small place to the next in your pet's natural habitat.

By establishing a gradient in the enclosure, your captive dragon will be able to access a range of different temperatures, which will allow him to manage his body temperature just as his wild counterparts do.

The need to establish a thermal gradient that varies about 20 degrees Fahrenheit (10 degrees Celsius) from one side to the other is one of the most compelling reasons to use a large cage. In general, the larger the cage, the easier it is to establish a suitable thermal gradient.

Overnight Temperatures

Bearded dragons should not be exposed to a constantly hot enclosure –
they need to cool off each night. Unless you are preparing the animals for
breeding trials, the basking lamps should be turned on for about 12 hours
each day, and turned off for the opposite 12 hours.

Because bearded dragon's safely tolerate temperatures in the high-60s
Fahrenheit (20 degrees Celsius) at night, most keepers can allow their
bearded dragon's habitat to fall to ambient room temperature at night.

Because it is important to avoid using lights on your dragon's habitat at
night, those living in homes with lower nighttime temperatures will need
to employ additional heat sources. Most such keepers accomplish this
through the use of ceramic heat emitters.

Ceramic heat emitters are small devices that function as light bulbs do,
except that they do not produce any visible light – they only produce heat.
While they are not an ideal heat source for your dragon's daytime basking
needs, they are very helpful for keeping your pet suitably warm at night.
You can use ceramic heat emitters in reflector-dome fixtures, just as you
would use incandescent bulbs.

Heating Equipment

Heat lamps are likely the best choices for supplying heat to your dragon.
Heat lamps consist of a reflector dome and an incandescent bulb. The light
bulb produces heat (in addition to light) and the metal reflector dome
directs the heat to a spot inside the cage.

You will need to clamp the lamp to a stable anchor or part of the cage's
frame. Always be sure that the lamp is securely attached and will not be
dislodged by vibration, children or pets.

Because fire safety is always a concern, and many keepers use high-
wattage lightbulbs, opt for heavy-duty reflector domes with ceramic bases,
rather than economy units with plastic bases. The price difference is
negligible, given the stakes.

One of the greatest benefits of using heat lamps to maintain the
temperature of your pet's habitat is the flexibility they offer. While you
can adjust the amount of heat provided by heat tapes and other devices
with a rheostat or thermostat, you can adjust the enclosure temperature
provided by heat lamps in two ways:

- **Changing the Bulb Wattage**

The simplest way to adjust the temperature of your dragon's cage is by changing the wattage of the bulb you are using.

For example, if a 40-watt light bulb is not raising the temperature of the basking spot high enough, you may try a 60-watt bulb. Alternatively, if a 100-watt light bulb is elevating the cage temperatures higher than are appropriate, switching to a 60-watt bulb may help.

- **Adjusting the Distance between the Heat Lamp and the Basking Spot**

The closer the heat lamp is to the cage, the warmer the cage will be. If the habitat is too warm, you can move the light farther from the enclosure, which should lower the basking spot temperatures slightly.

However, the farther away you move the lamp, the larger the basking spot becomes. It is important to be careful that you do not move it to far away, which will reduce the effectiveness of the thermal gradient by heating the enclosure too uniformly. In very large cages, this may not compromise the thermal gradient very much, but in a small cage, it may eliminate the "cool side" of the habitat. In other words, if your heat lamp creates a basking spot that is roughly 1-foot in diameter when it is 1inch away from the screen, it will produce a slightly cooler, but larger basking spot when moved back another 6 inches or so.

Thermometers

It is important to monitor the cage temperatures very carefully to ensure your pet stays health. Just as a water test kit is an aquarist's best friend, quality thermometers are some of the most important husbandry tools for reptile keepers.

Two different types of temperature are relevant for pet lizards: ambient temperatures and surface temperatures.

The ambient temperature in your animal's enclosure is the air temperature; the surface temperatures are the temperatures of the objects in the cage. Both are important to monitor, as they can differ widely.

For example, the air temperatures may be 90 degrees Fahrenheit (32 degrees Celsius) on a hot summer day, but the surface of a black rock may be in excess of 120 degrees Fahrenheit (48 degrees Celsius).

A lizard may comfortably rest on a branch with a surface temperature of 110 degrees Fahrenheit (43 degrees Celsius), but suffer from extreme heat stress if exposed to ambient temperatures in this range for very long.

Conversely, 150-degree ambient temperatures may be fatal, but they won't burn your lizard's skin. On the other hand, 150-degree surface temperatures may very well burn your pet's skin.

Measure the cage's ambient temperatures with a digital thermometer. An indoor-outdoor model will feature a probe that allows you to measure the temperature at both ends of the thermal gradient at once. For example, you may position the thermometer at the cool side of the cage, but attach the remote probe to a branch near the basking spot.

Because standard digital thermometers do not measure surface temperatures well, use a non-contact, infrared thermometer for such measurements. These devices will allow you to measure surface temperatures accurately from a short distance away.

Size-Related Heating Concerns

There is one more important factor to consider before you start devising the heating system for your bearded dragon's cage: Your lizard's body size influences the way in which he heats up and cools off.

Because volume increases more quickly than surface area does with increasing body size, small individuals experience more rapid temperature fluctuations than larger individuals do.

This principle is an especially important factor to keep in mind when caring for hatchling and juvenile dragons: Thermal stress affects such lizards quickly, and excessively high temperatures often prove fatal.

Accordingly, it is imperative to protect small individuals from temperature extremes. Conversely, larger dragons are more tolerant of temperature extremes than smaller individuals are.

Young bearded dragons often lie on top of one another when basking.

Chapter 8: Lighting the Enclosure

Given the amount of time they spend hanging out in the sun, it should come as no surprise that bearded dragons have evolved to depend upon it. It is always preferable to afford captive dragons access to unfiltered sunlight, but this is not always possible. In these cases, it is necessary to provide your dragon with high quality lighting, which can partially satisfy their need for real sunlight.

Dragons deprived of appropriate lighting may become seriously ill. Learning how to provide the proper lighting for reptiles is sometimes an arduous task for beginners, but it is very important to the long-term health of your pet that you do. To understand the type of light your lizard needs, you must first understand a little bit about light.

The Electromagnetic Spectrum

Light is a type of energy that physicists call electromagnetic radiation; it travels in waves. These waves may differ in amplitude, which correlates to the vertical distance between consecutive wave crests and troughs, frequency, which correlates with the number of crests per unit of time, and wavelength.

Wavelength is the distance from one crest to the next, or one trough to the next. Wavelength and frequency are inversely proportional, meaning that as the wavelength increases, the frequency decreases. It is more common for reptile keepers to discuss wavelengths rather than frequencies.

The sun produces energy (light) with a very wide range of constituent wavelengths. Some of these wavelengths fall within a range called the visible spectrum; humans can detect these rays with their eyes. Such waves have wavelengths between about 390 and 700 nanometers. Rays with wavelengths longer or shorter than these limits are broken into their own groups and given different names.

Those rays with around 390 nanometer wavelengths or less are called ultraviolet rays or UV rays. UV rays are broken down into three different categories, just as the different colors correspond with different wavelengths of visible light. UVA rays have wavelengths between 315 to 400 nanometers, while UVB rays have wavelengths between 280 and 315 nanometers while UVC rays have wavelengths between 100 and 280 nanometers.

Rays with wavelengths of less than 280 nanometers are called x-rays and gamma rays. At the other end of the spectrum, infrared rays have wavelengths longer than 700 nanometers; microwaves and radio waves are even longer.

UVA rays are important for food recognition, appetite, activity and eliciting natural behaviors. UVB rays are necessary for many reptiles to produce vitamin D3. Without this vitamin, reptiles cannot properly metabolize their calcium.

Light Color

The light that comes from the sun and light bulbs is composed of a combination of wavelengths, which create the blended white light that you perceive. This combination of wavelengths varies slightly from one light source to the next.

The sun produces very balanced white light, while "economy" incandescent bulbs produce relatively fewer blue rays and yields a yellow-looking light. High-quality bulbs designed for reptiles often produce very balanced, white light. The degree to which light causes objects to look as they would under sunlight is called the Color Rendering Index, or CRI. Sunlight has a CRI of 100, while quality bulbs have CRIs of 80 to 90; by contrast, a typical incandescent bulb has a CRI of 40 to 50

Light Brightness

Another important characteristic of light that relates to dragons is luminosity, or the brightness of light. Measured in units called Lux, luminosity is an important consideration for your lighting system. While you cannot possibly replicate the intensity of the sun's light, it is desirable in most circumstances to ensure the habitat is lit as well as is reasonably possible.

For example, in the tropics, the sunlight intensity averages around 100,000 Lux at midday; by comparison, the lights in a typical family living room only produce about 50 Lux.

Without bright lighting, many reptiles become lethargic, depressed or exhibit hibernating behaviors. Dim lighting may inhibit feeding and cause lizards to become stressed and ill.

Your Lizard's Lighting Needs

To reiterate, bearded dragons (and most other lizards) require:

- Light that is comprised of visible light, as well as UVA and UVB wavelengths

- Light with a high color-rendering index
- Light of the sufficiently strong intensity

Now that you know what your lizard requires, you can go about designing the lighting system for his habitat. Ultraviolet radiation is the most difficult component of proper lighting to provide, so it makes sense to begin by examining the types of bulbs that produce UV radiation.

The only commercially produced bulbs that produce significant amounts of UVA and UVB and suitable for a dragon habitat are linear fluorescent light bulbs, compact fluorescent light bulbs and mercury vapor bulbs.

Neither type of fluorescent bulb produces significant amounts of heat, but mercury vapor bulbs produce a lot of heat and serve a dual function. In many cases, keepers elect to use both types of lights – a mercury vapor bulb for a warm basking site with high levels of UV radiation and fluorescent bulbs to light the rest of the cage without raising the temperature. You can also use fluorescent bulbs to provide the requisite UV radiation and use a regular incandescent bulb to generate the basking spot.

Fluorescent bulbs have a much longer history of use than mercury vapor bulbs, which makes some keepers more comfortable using them. However, many models only produce moderate amounts of UVB radiation. While some mercury vapor bulbs produce significant quantities of UVB, some question the wisdom of producing more UV radiation than the animal receives in the wild. Additionally, mercury vapor bulbs are much too powerful to use in small habitats, and they are more expensive initially.

Most fluorescent bulbs must be placed within 12 inches of the basking surface, while some mercury vapor bulbs should be placed farther away from the basking surface – be sure to read the manufacturer's instructions before use. Be sure that the bulbs you purchase specifically state the amount of UVB radiation they produce; this figure is expressed as a percentage, for example 7% UVB. Most UVB-producing bulbs require replacement every six to 12 months – whether or not they have stopped producing light.

However, ultraviolet radiation is only one of the characteristics that lizard keepers must consider. The light bulbs used must also produce a sunlight-like spectrum. Fortunately, most high-quality light bulbs that produce significant amounts of UVA and UVB radiation also feature a high color-rendering index. The higher the CRI, the better, but any bulbs with a CRI of 90 or above will work well. If you are having trouble deciding between two otherwise evenly matched bulbs, select the one with the higher CRI value.

Brightness is the final, and easiest, consideration for the keeper to address. While no one yet knows what the ideal luminosity for a dragon's cage, it makes sense to ensure that at least part of the cage features very bright lighting. However, you should always offer a shaded retreat within the enclosure into which your lizard can avoid the light if he desires.

Connect the lights to an electric timer to keep the length of the day and night consistent. Some breeders manipulate their captive's photoperiod over the course of the year to prime the animals for breeding, but pet dragons thrive with 12 hours of daylight and 12 hours of darkness all year long.

Chapter 9: Substrate and Furniture

Once you have purchased or constructed your lizard's enclosure, you must place the appropriate items inside it. In general, these items take the form of an appropriate substrate and the proper cage furniture, including at least one perch.

Substrate

Substrate is a contentious issue among bearded dragon keepers. Some keepers utilize substrates similar to those used by keepers of other lizards, while others prefer to keep the cage floor bare. Both approaches have their merits.

Sand, Soil or Mixtures of the Two

Many different soils and sands make acceptable substrates for bearded dragons. You can dig up these materials yourself or purchase them from pet stores or garden supply retailers.

In all cases, the substrate materials must be free of pesticides, herbicides and other harmful chemicals. Additionally, you must avoid sands that are excessively abrasive or soils that are too rich in organic material.

Soil is a great substrate choice for those who intend to breed their dragons – if the moisture level is appropriate and the soil has enough depth, females will bury their eggs directly in the cage substrate. This alleviates the need for a separate egg-laying container.

Cypress Mulch

Cypress mulch is a popular substrate choice for bearded dragons. It not only looks attractive, but cypress mulch typically has a pleasant odor.

One drawback to cypress mulch is that some brands (or individual bags among otherwise good brands) produce a stick-like mulch, rather than mulch composed of thicker pieces. These sharp sticks can injure the keeper and the kept. It usually only takes one cypress mulch splinter jammed under a keeper's fingernail to cause them to switch substrates.

Cypress mulch is available from most home improvement and garden centers, as well as pet supply retailers. No matter the source you use, be sure that the product contains 100 percent cypress mulch without any demolition or salvage content.

Fir (Orchid) Bark

The bark of fir trees is often used for orchid propagation, and so it is often called "orchid bark." Orchid bark is very attractive, and, thanks to its relatively uniform shape, does not represent as much of an ingestion hazard as cypress mulch does. However, it is still wise to use a feeding cup if you elect to cover the bottom of the cage with this substrate.

Orchid bark absorbs water very well, so it is useful for species that require high humidity, such as bearded dragons. Additionally, orchid bark is easy to spot clean. However, monthly replacement can be expensive for those living in the Eastern United States and Europe.

Paper Products

Newspaper, paper towels and commercial cage liners are acceptable substrates for bearded dragons, and they are the preferred choice for hatchlings and lizards undergoing quarantine. Typically, you should use several pieces of paper to absorb any fluids your lizard may release.

Paper products are not very attractive, but they make it easy to keep the cage clean – you can simply remove the paper each day and replace it with a fresh sheet. Additionally, while you will have to purchase commercially produced cage liners, newspaper is essentially free.

However, paper substrates do present a few problems. Insects may crawl underneath the paper where they can hide from your lizard. Additionally, the ink from the paper can rub off on your lizard's feet and ventral surfaces.

Substrates to Avoid

Some substrates are completely inappropriate for dragon maintenance, and should be avoided at all costs. These include:

- **Aspen or Pine Shavings** – Wood shavings (as opposed to shredded bark or mulch) are not appropriate substrates for bearded dragons. In addition to representing a choking hazard, wood shavings will quickly rot if they become wet.

- **Cedar Shavings** – Cedar shavings produce toxic fumes that may sicken or kill your dragon. Always avoid cedar shavings.

- **Gravel** – You can use large gravel as a substrate, but its problems outweigh its benefits. Gravel must be washed when soiled, which is laborious and time consuming. Gravel is also quite heavy, which can cause headaches for the keeper.

- **Artificial Turf** – Although it seems like a viable option with a number of benefits, artificial turf is not a good substrate for dragons. Keeping artificial turf clean is difficult, and the threads may come loose and wrap around your lizard's tail, tongue or toes.

Cage Furniture

To complete your bearded dragon's habitat, you must provide him with visual barriers to help keep his stress level low, and perches on which he can bask. The easiest way to provide visual barriers for your dragon is by keeping live or fake plants in the enclosure.

Plants

Most keepers opt to use silk or plastic plants in their enclosures. This is a good option, but you must observe your lizard closely to ensure he or she does not attempt to eat the fake plants.

It is possible to use live plants in your bearded dragon's enclosure, but because you must ensure that the plants are not toxic to the animals and they survive in the enclosure, the options are relatively few.

Always wash all plants before placing them in the enclosure to help remove any pesticide residues. It is also wise to discard the potting soil used for the plant and replace it with fresh soil, which you know contains no pesticides, perlite or fertilizer.

While you can plant cage plants directly in soil substrates, this complicates maintenance and makes it difficult to replace the substrate regularly. Accordingly, it is generally preferable to keep the plant in some type of container.

Bearded dragons spend much of their time on elevated perches.

Perches

Bearded dragons need at least one perch in their habitat, but it is usually wise to provide two or three in total. Try to strike a good balance between offering your pet plenty of perches, without overly crowding the habitat.

Bearded dragons are skilled climbers, but they prefer very broad, flat branches and logs, as opposed to the thin branches preferred by chameleons and other tree-climbers.

Many different types of branches can be used in bearded dragon cages. Most non-aromatic hardwoods suffice. See the chart at the end of the chapter for specific recommendations.

You can purchase climbing branches from pet and craft stores, or you can collect them yourself. Try to use branches that are still attached to trees (always obtain permission first). Such branches will harbor fewer insects and other invertebrate pests than dead branches will.

Always wash branches with plenty of hot water and a stiff, metal-bristled scrub brush to remove as much dirt, dust and fungus as possible before placing them in your dragon's cage. Clean stubborn spots with a little bit of dish soap, but be sure to rinse them thoroughly afterwards.

Whether you purchased them from a pet store or collected them from the forest, it is advisable to sterilize all branches before placing them in a cage. The easiest way to do so is by placing the branch in a 300-degree oven for about 15 minutes. Doing so should kill the vast majority of pests and pathogens lurking inside the wood.

You can often place branches diagonally across the enclosure, in such a way that alleviates the need for direct attachment to the cage. However, horizontal branches will require secure points of attachment so they do not fall and injure your pet.

You can attach the branches to the cage in a variety of different ways. Be sure to make it easy to remove the branches as necessary, so you can clean them as necessary.

You can use hooks and eye-screws to suspend branches, which allows for quick and easy removal, but it is only applicable for cages with walls that will accept and support the eye-screws. You can also make "closet rod holders" by cutting a slot into small PVC caps, which are attached to the cage frame.

Recommended Species for Perches

Maple trees (*Acer* spp.)

Oak trees (*Quercus* spp.)

Walnut trees (*Juglans* spp.)

Ash trees (*Fraxinus* spp.)

Dogwood trees (*Cornus* spp.)

Sweetgum trees (*Liquidambar stryaciflua*)

Crepe Myrtle trees (*Lagerstroemia* spp.)

Willow trees (*Salix* spp.)

Tuliptrees (*Liriodendron tulipifera*)

Pear trees (*Pyrus* spp.)

Apple trees (*Malus* spp.)

Manzanitas (*Arctostaphylos* spp.)

Grapevine (*Vitis* spp.)

Species to Avoid

Cherry trees (*Prunus* spp.)

Pine trees (*Pinus* spp.)

Cedar trees (*Cedrus* spp., etc.)

Juniper trees (*Juniperus* spp.)

Poison ivy / oak (*Toxicodendron* spp.)

Chapter 10: Maintaining the Captive Habitat

Now that you have acquired your lizard and set up the enclosure, you must develop a protocol for maintaining his habitat. While dragon habitats require major maintenance every month or so, they only require minor daily maintenance.

In addition to designing a husbandry protocol, you must adopt a record-keeping system to track your dragon's growth and health.

Cleaning and Maintenance Procedures

Once you have decided on the proper enclosure for your pet, you must keep your lizard fed, hydrated and ensure that the habitat stays in proper working order to keep your captive healthy and comfortable.

Some tasks must be completed each day, while others are should be performed weekly, monthly or annually.

Daily
- Monitor the ambient and surface temperatures of the habitat.
- Provide drinking water (many keepers provide drinking water twice or thrice per day).
- Spot clean the cage to remove any loose insects, feces, urates or pieces of shed skin.
- Ensure that the lights, latches and other moving parts are in working order.
- Verify that your lizard is acting normally and appears healthy. You do not necessarily need to handle him to do so.
- Feed your lizard about 10 insects (some keepers only feed their captive five or six times per week).
- Ensure that the humidity and ventilation are at appropriate levels.

Weekly
- Change sheet-like substrates (newspaper, paper towels, etc.).
- Clean the inside surfaces of the enclosure.
- Inspect your lizard closely for any signs of injury, parasites or illness.
- Wash and sterilize all food dishes.

Monthly
- Break down the cage completely, remove and discard particulate substrates.

- Sterilize drip containers and similar equipment in a mild bleach solution.
- Measure and weigh your lizard.
- Photograph your pet (recommended, but not imperative).
- Prune any plants as necessary.

Annually
- Replace the batteries in your thermometers and any other devices that use them.
- Replace any UVB-producing bulbs (some must be changed every six months).

Cleaning your lizard's cage and furniture is relatively simple. Regardless of the way it became soiled, the basic process remains the same:

1. Rinse the object
2. Using a scrub brush or sponge and soapy water, remove any organic debris from the object.
3. Rinse the object thoroughly.
4. Disinfect the object.
5. Re-rinse the object.
6. Dry the object.

Chemicals & Tools
A variety of chemicals and tools are necessary for reptile care. Save yourself some time by purchasing dedicated cleaning products and keeping them in the same place that you keep your tools.

Spray Bottles
Misting your dragon and his habitat with fresh water is one of the best ways to provide him with water. You can do this with a small, handheld misting bottle or a larger, pressurized unit (such as those used to spray herbicides). Automated units are available, but they are rarely cost-effective unless you are caring for a large colony of lizards.

Scrub Brushes or Sponges
It helps to have a few different types of scrub brushes and sponges on hand for scrubbing and cleaning different items. Use the least abrasive sponge or brush suitable for the task to prevent wearing out cage items prematurely. Do not use abrasive materials on glass or acrylic surfaces. Steel-bristled brushes work well for scrubbing coarse, wooden items, such as branches.

Spatulas and Putty Knives
Spatulas, putty knives and similar tools are often helpful for cleaning reptile cages. For example, urates (which are not soluble in anything short of hot lava) often become stuck on cage walls or furniture. Instead of trying to dissolve them with harsh chemicals, just scrape them away with a sturdy plastic putty knife.

Small Vacuums
Small, handheld vacuums are very helpful for sucking up the dust left behind from substrates. They are also helpful for cleaning the cracks and crevices around the cage doors. A shop vacuum, with suitable hoses and attachments, can also be helpful.

Steam Cleaners
Steam cleaners are very effective for sterilizing cages, water bowls and durable cage props after they have been cleaned. In fact, steam is often a better choice than chemical disinfectants, as it will not leave behind a toxic residue. Never use a steam cleaner near your lizard, the plants in his cage or any other living organisms.

Soap
Use a gentle, non-scented dish soap. Antibacterial soap is preferred, but not necessary. Most people use far more soap than is necessary -- a few drops mixed with a quantity of water is usually sufficient to help remove surface pollutants.

Bleach
Bleach (diluted to one-half cup per gallon of water) makes an excellent disinfectant. Be careful not to spill any on clothing, carpets or furniture, as it is likely to discolor the objects.

Always be sure to rinse objects thoroughly after using bleach and be sure that you cannot detect any residual odor. Bleach does not work as a disinfectant when in contact with organic substances; accordingly, items must be cleaned before you can disinfect them.

Veterinarian Approved Disinfectant
Many commercial products are available that are designed to be safe for their pets. Consult with your veterinarian about the best product for your situation, its method of use and its proper dilution.

Avoid Phenols
Always avoid cleaners that contain phenols, as they are extremely toxic to some reptiles. In general, do not use household cleaning products to avoid exposing your pet to toxic chemicals.

Keeping Records

It is important to keep records regarding your pet's health, growth and feeding, as well as any other important details. In the past, reptile keepers would do so on small index cards or in a notebook. In the modern world, technological solutions may be easier. For example, you can use your computer or mobile device to keep track of the pertinent info about your pet.

You can record as much information about your pet as you like, and the more information to you record, the better. But minimally, you should record the following:

Pedigree and Origin Information
Be sure to record the source of your lizard, the date on which you acquired him and any other data that is available. Breeders will often provide customers with information regarding the sire, dam, date of birth, weights and feeding records, but other sources will rarely offer comparable data.

Feeding Information
Record the date of each feeding (and time of day, if you feed more than once each day), as well as the type of food item(s) offered. It is also helpful to record any preferences you may observe or any meals that are refused.

Weights and Length
Because you look at your pet frequently, it is difficult to appreciate how quickly he is (or isn't) growing. Accordingly, it is important to track his size diligently.

Weigh bearded dragons with a high quality digital scale. The scale must be sensitive to one-tenth-gram increments to be useful for very small lizards.

You can measure your lizard's length as well, but this should be viewed as a supplemental measurement – your pet's weight is a better indicator of health and a more accurate measure of your lizard's growth.

Maintenance Information
Record all of the noteworthy events associated with your pet's care. While it is not necessary to note that you misted the cage each day, it is appropriate to record the dates on which you changed the substrate or sterilized the cage.

Whenever you purchase new equipment, supplies or caging, note the date and source. This helps to remind you when you purchased the items, but it may help you track down a source for the items in the future, if necessary.

Breeding Information

If you intend to breed your lizard, you should record all details associated with pre-breeding conditioning, cycling, introductions, copulations, color changes, copulations and egg deposition.

Record all pertinent information about any resulting clutches as well, including the number of viable eggs, as well as the number of unhatched and unfertilized eggs (often called "slugs" by reptile keepers).

Record Keeping Samples

The following are two different examples of suitable recording systems.

The first example is reminiscent of the style employed by many with large collections. Because such keepers often have numerous animals, the notes are very simple, and require a minimum amount of writing or typing.

ID Number: 44522		Genus: Species/Sub:	Pogona vitticeps	Gender: DOB:	Male 3/20/15	CARD #2
6.30.15 Crickets, Collard Greens	7.03.15 Crickets, 1 Small Roach	7.07.15 Large Roach, Collard Greens	7.14.15 Shed Skin	7.17.15 Crickets, Collard Greens		
7.01.15 Crickets, Collard Greens	7.05.15 Crickets, Collard Greens	7.08.15 Roaches	7.15.15 Small Mealworms	7.19.15 Sterilized Cage		
7.02.15 Roaches	7.06.15 Crickets, Collard Greens	7.10.15 Crickets, Collard Greens	7.16.15 Crickets, Collard Greens			

The second example demonstrates a simple approach that is employed by many with small collections (or a single pet): keeping notes on paper. Such notes could be taken in a notebook or journal, or you could type directly into a word processor. It does not matter *how* you keep records, just that you *do* keep records.

Date	Notes
6-25-13	Acquired "Drogo" the bearded dragon from a lizard breeder named Mark at the in-town reptile expo. Mark explained that Drogo's scientific name is Pogona vitticeps. Cost was $250. Mark said that Drogo is a boy. Mark said he purchased him in March, but he does not know the exact date.
6-26-13	Drogo spent the night in the container I bought him in. I purchased a small aquarium, full spectrum lamp and heat lamp at the pet store. I bought the thermometer at the hardware store next door and ordered a non-contact thermometer online. I added a large branch I found outside so he can climb.
6-27-13	Drogo eagerly drank when I misted him. He also ate 10 crickets. It's funny watching him try to catch them!
6-29-13	I fed Drogo 10 crickets and a big roach today. He still looked kinda hungry, but I think that was enough for the day.
7-1-13	I fed Drogo three roaches today. I think he likes roaches more than crickets, but I will keep giving him a mix of both.
7-3-13	I tried to give Drogo some collard greens today, but he didn't seem interested. He did eat a few crickets though, so maybe he just doesn't like vegetables yet.

Chapter 11: Feeding Bearded Dragons

Like most other dragons, bearded dragons primarily feed on invertebrates and vegetation.

The best captive diet for bearded dragons is one that mimics their wild diet, being primarily comprised of gut-loaded insects, supplemented with plenty of leafy green vegetables. It is not necessary to feed bearded dragons any vertebrate prey, although some keepers offer the occasional newborn mouse to mature dragons.

Like most other species, bearded dragons benefit from a varied diet, which helps to minimize the effects of dietary excess and vitamin and mineral deficiencies. However, providing a varied diet is not always sufficient to avoid deficiencies, so it is wise to supplement some of your pet's food with additional vitamins and minerals.

Insects

Insects should form the bulk of the diet for bearded dragons of all sizes. Crickets or roaches make a nice staple, while the other insects can be incorporated to add variety. Some keepers supplement their captive's diet with wild caught insects, but discretion is advised, as such insects may be contaminated with pesticides or infested with parasites.

Bearded dragons often use their tongue to catch insects.

The following insects make suitable prey for bearded dragons:

- Crickets

- Roaches
- Mealworms
- Giant mealworms
- Super worms
- Wax worms
- Grasshoppers

Other Invertebrates

Aside from insects, a number of invertebrates make suitable food sources for bearded dragons. However, few are available commercially, so they rarely form more than a trivial portion of a captive dragon's diet. A few examples of acceptable invertebrates include:

- Earthworms
- Snails
- Slugs
- Roly polies

Vertebrates

In the wild, bearded dragons occasionally consume small lizards or snakes. While your bearded dragon will remain perfectly healthy without eating any vertebrate prey, it is probably not a problem to offer the occasional newborn mouse to your pet. However, too many rodents will quickly cause your dragon to become obese and suffer from serious health problems.

If you choose to offer rodents to your pet, offer pre-killed, rather than live, individuals, to avoid any suffering on the part of the rodent. Live newborn rodents will not harm your lizard, but it is important to treat all feeder animals with respect, and avoid any unnecessary suffering.

Neither lizards nor snakes should be offered as prey, as they are likely to be infested with parasites, which they may transmit to your pet.

Prey Size

Mature bearded dragons can easily handle and consume relatively large insects; adult crickets and large roaches are rarely a problem.

Juveniles, by contrast, are much too small to consume large insects. In fact, feeding large insects to small dragons can cause them to become impacted. In some cases, this can be fatal. To avoid such eventualities, offer small dragons insects that are no longer than the distance between the lizard's eyes.

How to Offer Food

Unless you use a cage with an exceptionally tight mesh, you cannot simply dump a handful of crickets or roaches in your bearded dragon's cage. While your pet may be able to snatch one or two of the insects, the majority will simply crawl out of the cage and into your home.

This leaves keepers with one of two options. You can either offer insects individually by hand or via forceps; or you can use a feeding cup, which will keep the insects contained. Hand feeding is laborious, but acceptable if you do not mind devoting this amount of time to your pet's daily feedings.

If you elect to use a feeding cup, you will need to select a cup that is tall enough to keep the insects contained, and yet short enough that the lizard can reach them via his tongue. Alternatively, if the mouth of the cup is wide enough to accommodate the lizard's body, you can arrange a perch that allows the lizard to get close enough to the insects to reach them.

You can allow insects to sit in the feeding cup for about 24 hours, but do not let them sit in here for any longer. Clean the feeding cup daily with soap and water, and disinfect it periodically.

Feeding Quantity and Frequency

Offer mature dragons food every day or every other day. Provide your pet with as many insects as he will eat in about 10 minutes. If you wish, you can offer a second meal later that day.

Young bearded dragons will benefit from slightly smaller, yet more frequent meals. Accordingly, feed young dragons as many insects as they will eat in 2 or 3 minutes, but provide them with two or three daily meals.

Always remove any uneaten insects after the allotted time to prevent them from harming your pet.

Fruits and Vegetables

Although bearded dragons consume a significant quantity of insects and other invertebrates, vegetation plays an important role in their diets as well. In addition to being rich in vitamins and minerals, most plant material is full of water, which will help keep your dragon hydrated.

Dark leafy greens are the best vegetables to offer your lizard. You can simply keep a leaf suspended in the cage and allow your dragon to munch on it as he desires. Be sure to place it near a perch so that your lizard can access it easily. Misting the leaf may catch his attention and stimulate his interest in the food. Remove and replace the leaf after about 24 hours to prevent it from spoiling.

In addition to leafy greens, you can also provide your pet with a number of other fruits and vegetables (see chart). You can leave any leafs uncut, just be sure to attach them securely to the cage or a favorite perch, so the lizard can rip off small pieces. Vegetable-based foods that cannot be used in this fashion should be cut into small pieces or grated, and placed on a plate.

A twice- or thrice-weekly offering of plant material is likely sufficient for your pet's health, but there is little downside to offering vegetables and fruits more often than this, if your pet is interested. Young bearded dragons may show less interest in vegetables than adults do, but continue to offer them to your pet to instill good eating habits.

Some bearded dragons relish flower petals.

Listed below are a few foods that you can offer to your dragon, which are widely agreed to be safe. Remember that your lizard is an individual, with his own unique preferences and favorites – he may like some and avoid others.

Always wash all fruits and vegetables before offering them to your pet, to help remove any waxes or pesticides.

Collard greens

Turnip greens

Mustard greens

Dandelions

Grape leaves

Hibiscus

Roses

Cilantro

Parsley

Endive

Kale

Broccoli

Carrots

Squash

Zucchini

Pumpkin

Kiwi

Strawberries

Blueberries

Blackberries

Apples

Pears

Vitamin and Mineral Supplements

Many keepers add commercially produced vitamin and mineral supplements to their dragon's food on a regular basis. In theory, these supplements help to correct dietary deficiencies and ensure that captive lizards get a balanced diet. In practice, things are not this simple.

While some vitamins and minerals are unlikely to build up to toxic levels, others may very well cause problems if provided in excess. This means that you cannot simply apply supplements to every meal – you must decide upon a sensible supplementation schedule.

Additionally, it can be difficult to ascertain exactly how much of the various vitamins and minerals you will be providing to your lizard, as most such products are sold as fine powders, designed to be sprinkled on feeder insects. This is hardly a precise way to provide the proper dose to your lizard, and the potential for grossly over- or under-estimating the amount of supplement delivered is very real.

Because the age, sex and health of your dragon all influence the amount of vitamins and minerals your pet requires, and each individual product has a unique composition, it is wise to consult your veterinarian before deciding upon a supplementation schedule. However, most keepers provide vitamin supplementation once each week, and calcium supplementation several times per week.

Chapter 12: Providing Water to Your Bearded Dragon

Bearded dragons have adapted to life in the arid regions of Australia, where standing water is scarce. Nevertheless, like most other animals, bearded dragons require drinking water to remain healthy.

Providing Drinking Water

Providing ample drinking water is imperative to the health of your bearded dragon. Be sure to provide drinking water at least once each day, whether or not your lizard drinks any. This is especially important for young dragons, whose surface-to-volume ratio causes them to dehydrate more rapidly than adults do.

Providing drinking water to a bearded dragon requires some ingenuity, as some individuals fail to recognize standing water for what it is. Instead of drinking from a water dish, most bearded dragons prefer to drink droplets of water dripping from their bodies or the cage furniture.

The easiest way to provide water in this way is by misting the dragon, the perches and any plants inside the enclosure. The resulting water droplets will usually entice your dragon to lap them up greedily.

You can mist the cage with a hand-held misting bottle, a pressurized unit or an automated misting system. An inexpensive hand-held misting bottle usually suffices for those caring for a single dragon, while those maintaining several individuals often find the latter two options more efficient.

Nevertheless, some bearded dragons (particularly adults) can learn to drink from a water dish, which makes maintenance much easier for the keeper. It is usually preferable to offer water for about 1 hour at a time before removing it until the next day. This prevents the animals from fouling the water and then ingesting bacteria or parasites.

Some keepers prefer to give their dragon dechlorinated or purified or spring water, but others simply offer tap water. Purified bottled water and spring water are typically safe for dragons, but distilled water should be avoided to prevent causing electrolyte imbalances.

It is wise to have tap water tested to ensure that heavy metals or other pollutants are not present before offering it to your dragon.

Soaking

In addition to providing drinking water, many keepers soak their bearded dragons periodically in a tub of clean, lukewarm water. Soaking is helpful tool for the husbandry of many reptiles, even those who hail from arid habitats.

In addition to ensuring that your pet remains adequately hydrated, soaks help to remove dirt and encourage complete, problem-free sheds. It is not necessary to soak your lizard if it remains adequately hydrated, but most benefit from an occasional soak.

Soaks should last a maximum of about one hour, and be performed no more often than once per week (unless the lizard is experiencing shedding difficulties).

When soaking your pet, the water should not be very deep. Never make your lizard swim to keep its head above water. Ideally, bearded dragons should be soaked in containers with only enough water to cover their back. This should allow them to rest comfortably with its head above water.

Never leave your pet unattended while it is soaking. If your bearded dragon defecates in the water, be sure to rinse him off with clean water before returning him to his cage.

Humidity

Bearded dragons hail from habitats with a very low humidity for most of the year. Strive to keep their enclosure similarly dry to prevent your lizards from contracting respiratory infections and other problems.

As long as the habitat provides good ventilation, it will usually remain dry enough to keep your lizards healthy. Avoid leaving a large water dish in the cage at all times and be sure that the cage dries within a few hours of being misted.

Some substrates – particularly cypress mulch – contain a great deal of moisture when first purchased. As long as the substrate dries over the course of a day or two, this is no cause for concern. However, if the substrate is particularly damp, you should let it sit outside in the sun until it dries.

Chapter 13: Interacting with Your Pet

While bearded dragons are not very social animals, and your pet will never suffer from a lack of human interaction, most individuals will tolerate brief, gentle handling.

Handling Your Bearded Dragon

The very best way to handle your dragon is try to slide your hand (or finger, in the case of small individuals) underneath his chin and gently begin lifting him up. This will normally cause your lizard to crawl into your hand voluntarily.

Hold your bearded dragon gently in your hand, and place your thumb lightly on his back to prevent him from leaping off suddenly. Use care to avoid squeezing your dragon, as this will cause him to feel threatened, making him squirm to escape.

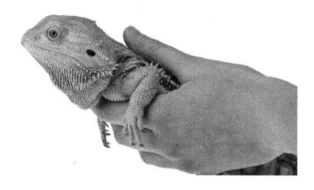

Support your pet to keep him calm and relaxed.

Never lift a bearded dragon by the tail or the limbs, as this could lead to injuries.

Aggressive Dragons

Dragons are not typically considered "aggressive" or "dangerous" lizards, but some individuals do respond poorly to their keeper's advances. Most individuals will simply attempt to flee when approached, while others may exhibit darkened colors or gape at the perceived threat. Some are even willing to bite, should their keeper not heed these warnings.

There is often little that the keeper can do to change the attitude of such pets. Keeping your lizard's stress level low and providing proper husbandry may help. Additionally, you may be able to calm your lizard over time, via repeated, brief and gentle interactions.

In the event of a bearded dragon bite, try to remain calm. Bites from bearded dragons are akin to a strong pinch, and they rarely cause any serious damage (obviously, it is wise to keep your dragon away from your face as bites here could be more serious).

Usually bearded dragons release their bite fairly quickly. If they do not, it is usually possible to pry their mouth open with a credit card or similar object. A soft plastic spatula is an ideal tool for this task, as the flexible blade is unlikely to injure your pet.

Transporting Your Pet

Although you should strive to avoid any unnecessary travel with your lizard, circumstances often demand that you do (such as when your lizard becomes ill).

Strive to make the journey as stress-free as possible for your pet. This means protecting him from physical harm, as well as blocking as much stressful stimuli as possible.

The best type of container to use when transporting your dragon is a plastic storage box or small, screened cage. Add several ventilation holes to plastic containers to provide suitable ventilation.

If the trip is to be brief, the added security, protection and thermal stability of a plastic storage box is generally preferable to the screened container. Conversely, the improved air exchange offered by a screened cage will prove beneficial on long journeys.

Place a few paper towels or some clean newspaper in the bottom of the box to absorb any fluids, should your lizard defecate or discharge urates. You can add a few plant cuttings to the cage to provide cover for your pet, but it is not strictly necessary.

Cover the outside of his transportation cage if you are not using an opaque container. This will prevent your pet from seeing the chaos occurring outside his container. Monitor your lizard regularly, but avoid constantly opening the container to take a peak. Checking up on your pet once every half-hour or so is more than sufficient.

Pay special attention to the enclosure temperatures while traveling. Use your digital thermometer to monitor the air temperatures inside the transportation container. Try to keep the temperatures in the low 80s Fahrenheit (26 to 29 degrees Celsius) so that your pet will remain comfortable. Use the air-conditioning or heater in your vehicle as needed to keep the animal within this range.

Do not jostle your pet unnecessarily and always use a gentle touch when moving the container. Never leave the container unattended.

Hygiene

Reptiles can carry *Salmonella* spp., *Escherichia coli* and several other zoonotic pathogens. Accordingly, it is imperative that you use good hygiene practices when handling reptiles.

Always wash your hands with soap and warm water each time you touch your pet, his habitat or the tools you use to care for him. Antibacterial soaps are preferred, but standard hand soap will suffice.

In addition to keeping your hands clean, you must also take steps to ensure *your* environment does not become contaminated with pathogens. In general, this means keeping your lizard and any of the tools and equipment you use to maintain his habitat separated from your belongings.

Establish a safe place for preparing his food, storing equipment and cleaning his habitat. Make sure these places are far from the places in which you prepare your food and personal effects. Never wash cages or tools in kitchens or bathrooms that are used by humans.

Always clean and sterilize any items that become contaminated by the germs from your lizard or his habitat.

Chapter 14: Common Health Concerns

Your dragon cannot tell you when he is sick; dragons endure illness stoically. This does not mean that injuries and illnesses do not cause them distress, but without expressive facial features, they do not *look* like they are suffering.

In fact, reptiles typically do not display symptoms until the disease has already reached an advanced state. Accordingly, it is important to treat injuries and illnesses promptly – often with the help of a qualified veterinarian –in order to provide your pet with the best chance of recovery.

Finding a Suitable Veterinarian

Dragon keepers often find that it is more difficult to find a veterinarian to treat their lizard than it is to find a vet to treat a cat or dog. Relatively few veterinarians treat reptiles, so it is important to find a reptile-oriented vet *before* you need one. There are a number of ways to do this:

- You can search veterinarian databases to find one that is local and treats reptiles.
- You can inquire with your dog or cat vet to see if he or she knows a qualified reptile-oriented veterinarian to whom he or she can refer you.
- You can contact a local reptile-enthusiast group or club. Most such organizations will be familiar with the local veterinarians.
- You can inquire with local nature preserves or zoos. Most will have relationships with veterinarians that treat reptiles and other exotic animals.

Those living in major metropolitan areas may find a vet reasonably close, but rural reptile keepers may have to travel considerable distances to find veterinary assistance.

If you do not have a reptile-oriented veterinarian within driving distance, you can try to find a conventional veterinarian who is willing to consult with a reptile-oriented veterinarian via the phone or internet. These types of "two-for-one" visits may be expensive, as you will have to pay for both the actual visit and the consultation, but they may be your only option.

Reasons to Visit the Veterinarian

While reptiles do not require vaccinations or similar routine treatments, they may require visits to treat illnesses or injuries. However, you needn't travel to the vet every time your dragon refuses a meal or experiences a bad shed. In fact, unnecessary veterinary visits may prove more harmful than helpful, so it is important to distinguish between those ailments that require care and those that are best treated at home.

When in doubt, contact your veterinarian and solicit his or her advice before packing up your lizard and hauling him in for an office visit. However, any of the following signs or symptoms can indicate serious problems, and each requires veterinary evaluation.

Visit your veterinarian when:

- Anytime your lizard wheezes, exhibits labored breathing or produces a mucus discharge from its nostrils or mouth.
- Your lizard produces soft or watery feces for longer than 48 hours.
- He suffers any significant injury. Common examples include thermal burns, friction damage to the rostral (nose) region or injured feet.
- Reproductive issues occur, such as being unable to deliver eggs. If a lizard appears nervous, agitated or otherwise stressed and unable to expel eggs, see your veterinarian immediately.
- Your lizard fails to feed for an extended period (more than three or four days).
- Your lizard displays any unusual lumps, bumps or lesions.
- Your lizard's intestines prolapse.

Ultimately, you must make all the decisions on behalf of your lizard, so weigh the pros and cons of each veterinary trip carefully and make the best decision you can for your pet. Just be sure that you always strive to act in his best interest.

Common Health Problems

The following are a few of the most common health problems that afflict bearded dragons. Their causes and the suggested course of action are also discussed.

Retained or Poor Sheds

Dragons do not shed their entire skin at one time, as snakes do. Instead, they tend to shed in numerous pieces, over several hours or days. Occasionally, this can cause them to retain portions of their old skin. While this is not usually a big problem, care must be taken to ensure that the face, tail tip and toes all shed completely. If skin is retained in these places, blood flow can be restricted, eventually causing the death of the associated tissues. Sometimes this leads to the loss of toes or tail tips.

The best way to remove retained sheds is by temporarily increasing the enclosure humidity and misting your animal more frequently. In cases involving small amounts of retained skin, this may be enough to resolve the problem within a few days.

If this does not work, you may need to remove the retained skin manually. If the skin is partially free, you can try to get a grip on the loose part and gently pull the remaining skin free (do not try this if the retained skin attaches near the eyes).

If the retained skin is not peeling up around the edges, you will not be able to grip it. In such cases, use a damp paper towel to gently rub the area in question. With a little bit of water and gentle friction, you can usually dislodge the retained skin.

Always avoid forcing the skin off, as you may injure your pet. If the skin does not come off easily, return him to his cage and try again in 12 to 24 hours. Usually, repeated dampening will loosen the skin sufficiently to be removed.

If repeated treatments do not yield results, consult your veterinarian. He may feel that the retained shed is not causing a problem, and advise you to leave it attached – it should come off with the next shed. Alternatively, it if is causing a problem, the veterinarian can remove it without much risk of harming your pet.

Respiratory Infections
Like humans, lizards can suffer from respiratory infections. Dragons with respiratory infections exhibit fluid or mucus draining from their nose and/or mouth, may be lethargic and are unlikely to eat. They may also spend excessive amounts of time basking on or under the heat source, in an effort to induce a "behavioral fever."

Bacteria, or, less frequently, fungi or parasites often cause respiratory infections. In addition, cleaning products, perfumes, pet dander and other particulate matter can irritate a reptile's respiratory tract as well. Some such bacteria and most fungi are ubiquitous, and only become problematic when they overwhelm an animal's immune system. Other bacteria and most viruses are transmitted from one lizard to another.

To reduce the chances of illnesses, keep your lizard separated from other lizards, keep his enclosure exceptionally clean and be sure to provide the best husbandry possible, in terms of temperature, ventilation and humidity. Additionally, avoid stressing your pet by handling him too frequently, or exposing him to chaotic situations.

Veterinary care is almost always required to treat respiratory infections. Your vet will likely take samples of the mucus and have it analyzed to determine the causal agent. The veterinarian will then prescribe medications, if appropriate, such as antibiotics.

It is imperative to carry out the actions prescribed by your veterinarian exactly as stated, and keep your lizard's stress level very low while he is healing. Stress can reduce immune function, so avoid handling him unnecessarily, and consider covering the front of his cage while he recovers.

"Mouth Rot"
Mouth rot – properly called stomatitis – is identified by noting discoloration, discharge or cheesy-looking material in your dragon's mouth. Mouth rot can be a serious illness, and requires the attention of your veterinarian.

While mouth rot can follow an injury (such as happens when a lizard rubs his snout against the sides of the cage) it can also arise from systemic illness. Your veterinarian will cleanse your lizard's mouth and potentially prescribe an antibiotic.

Your veterinarian may recommend withholding food until the problem is remedied. Always be sure that lizards recovering from mouth rot have immaculately clean habitats, with appropriate temperature, humidity and ventilation, as well as ideal temperatures.

By virtue of the way their teeth attach to the jaw bone (termed acrodont dentition), bearded dragons are especially susceptible to periodontal disease. This can be painful for the lizard and difficult to treat, so it is important to avoid the problem entirely.

Unfortunately, this is not always easy to accomplish. The most important way you can provide your lizards with some protection from periodontal disease is through a combination of the proper diet, access to suitable temperatures and keeping the enclosure very clean.

Internal Parasites
In the wild, most dragons carry some internal parasites. While it may not be possible to keep a reptile completely free of internal parasites, it is important to keep these levels in check.

Consider any wild-caught animals to be parasitized until proven otherwise. While most captive bred dragons should have relatively few internal parasites, they are not immune to them.

Preventing parasites from building to pathogenic levels requires strict hygiene. Many parasites build up to dangerous levels when lizards are kept in cages that are continuously contaminated from feces.

Most internal parasites that are of importance for lizards are transmitted via the fecal-oral route. This means that eggs (or a similar life stage) of the parasites are released with the feces. If the lizard inadvertently ingests these, the parasites can develop inside his body and cause increased problems.

Parasite eggs are usually microscopic and easily carried by gentle drafts, where they may stick to cage walls or land in the feeding dish. Later, when the dragon snaps up an insect from the feeding dish, he ingests the eggs as well.

Internal parasites may cause your lizard to vomit, pass loose stools, fail to grow or refuse food entirely. Other parasites may produce no obvious symptoms at all, despite causing considerable damage to your pet's internal organs. This illustrates the importance of routine fecal examinations (which do not necessarily require that you bring your pet into the office).

Your veterinarian will usually examine your pet's feces if he suspects internal parasites. By looking at the type of eggs inside the feces, your veterinarian can prescribe an appropriate medication. Many parasites are easily treated with anti-parasitic medications, but often, these medications must be given several times to eradicate the pathogens completely.

Some parasites may be transmissible to people, so always take proper precautions, including regular hand washing and keeping reptiles and their cages away from kitchens and other areas where foods are prepared.

Examples of common internal parasites include roundworms, tapeworms and amoebas.

External Parasites
Dragons can theoretically suffer from external parasites, such as ticks and mites, but this appears to be a relatively rare occurrence.

Ticks should be removed manually. Using tweezers grasp the tick as close as possible to the lizard's skin and pull with steady, gentle pressure. Do not place anything over the tick first, such as petroleum jelly, or carry out any other "home remedies," such as burning the tick with a match. Such techniques may cause the tick to inject more saliva (which may contain diseases or bacteria) into the dragon's body.

Drop the tick in a jar of isopropyl alcohol to kill it. It is a good idea to bring these to your veterinarian for analysis. Do not contact ticks with your bare hands, as many species can transmit disease to humans.

Mites are another matter entirely. While ticks are generally large enough to see easily, mites are about the size of a pepper flake. Whereas tick infestations usually only tally a few individuals, mite infestations may include thousands of individual parasites.

Mites may afflict wild caught lizards, but, as they are not confined to a small cage, such infestations are usually self-limiting. However, in captivity, mite infestations can approach plague proportions.

After a female mite feeds on a lizard, she drops off and finds a safe place (such as a tiny crack in a cage or among the substrate) to deposit her eggs. After the eggs hatch, they travel back to your pet (or to other lizards in your collection) where they feed and perpetuate the lifecycle.

Whereas a few mites may represent little more than an inconvenience to the lizard, a significant infection stresses them considerably, and may even cause death through anemia. This is particularly true for small or young animals. Additionally, mites may transmit disease from one animal to another.

There are a number of different methods for eradicating a mite infestation. In each case, there are two primary steps that must be taken: You must eradicate the lizard's parasites as well as the parasites in the environment (which includes the room in which the cage resides).

Soaking is often a strategy for ridding a lizard of mites, but it is not a viable option for dragons. In most cases a chemical treatment will be necessary. Consult with your veterinarian, who can recommend a prudent treatment.

You will also need to perform a thorough cage cleaning to eliminate the problem. To do so, you must remove everything from the cage, including water dishes, substrates and cage props. Sterilize all impermeable cage items, and discard the substrate and all porous cage props – including plants and trees. Vacuum the area around the cage and wipe down all of the nearby surfaces with a wet cloth.

It may be necessary to repeat this process several times to eradicate the mites completely. Accordingly, the very best strategy is to avoid contracting mites in the first place. This is why it is important to purchase your dragon from a reliable breeder or retailer, and keep him quarantined from potential mite vectors.

Long-Term Anorexia
While dragons may refuse the occasional meal, they should not fast for prolonged periods of time.

The most common reasons that dragons refuse food are improper temperatures and illness. Parasites and bacterial infections can also cause dragons to refuse food. Consult your veterinarian anytime that your lizard refuses food for longer than three or four days.

Chapter 15: Breeding Bearded dragons

Reproduction among captive dragons has become more common over the last few decades, and bearded dragons are one of the most frequently bred lizard species.

This is very fortunate for prospective keepers; captive bred bearded dragons make better pets than wild caught specimens do. Breeding bearded dragons is a relatively straightforward process, and requires only a few basic steps to complete.

Sexing Bearded Dragons

Adult bearded dragons exhibit a variety of secondary sexual characteristics that help distinguish males from females. Males usually reach larger sizes than females do and have shorter, stockier bodies. Additionally, males often possess much larger heads and more prominent femoral pores than females do.

However, the most definitive clues can be found on the underside of your bearded dragon's tail base. Begin by resting your lizard on your palm, with its head facing away from you. Gently grip your lizard's tail and arch it over the back. If it is a male, you should be able to see its hemipenes on both sides of the tail, right behind the vent. Females, by contrast, have no such bulges. Sometimes it is easiest to see the bulges by gently twisting the tail from side to side, while looking for the bulges.

Hemipenal bulges are the only reliable way of sexing you bearded dragons, but it is much more difficult to distinguish between the sexes when the animals are young. However, it becomes pretty easy to sex them by the time they are about 12 weeks of age. Experienced breeders can often discern a dragon's sex long before this.

Pre-Breeding Conditioning

Breeding reptiles always entails risk, so it is wise to refrain from breeding any animals that are not in excellent health. Breeding is especially stressful for female dragons, who must withstand potential injuries during mating, and produce numerous, nutrient-rich eggs.

Animals slated for breeding trials must have excellent body weight, but obesity is to be avoided, as it is associated with reproductive problems. Ensure that the lizards are appropriately hydrated, and are free of parasites, infections and injuries.

Cycling

Cycling is the terms used to describe the climactic changes keepers impose upon their animals. These changes are intended to mimic the natural seasonal changes in an animal's natural habitat.

Bearded dragon keepers seeking to breed their animals often simulate winter conditions by reducing the enclosure temperatures and providing fewer hours of lighting for a period of 1 to 3 months. Generally, by shifting from 12 to 14 hours of light, cycling regimens call for only 4 to 6 hours of light each day. When the lights are off, the cage temperatures are allowed to fall to the ambient temperature of the room.

These changes may not be strictly necessary for stimulating bearded dragons to breed, but it is generally beneficial for breeding efforts. Nevertheless, many breeders have had success without using a cycling regimen at all.

It is important to reduce the temperatures and photoperiod gradually to avoid stressing the animals. Additionally, food should be withheld during the cycling period. Provide water to the animals periodically to avoid dehydration.

At the end of the cycling period, begin restoring the lights and temperatures to their normal level. Begin feeding the animals as soon as they will start eating. It is important that they feed well before breeding trials commence.

Breeding Trials

Once the bearded dragons have had a few weeks to feed following cycling, breeding trials can begin.

If you maintain the animals together all year long, copulations will likely occur without any additional effort on your part. If you keep the animals separately for most of the year, this is the time to introduce them to each other.

Most breeders using this method introduce males into the cages of their female counterparts, but the opposite strategy can be just as effective.

Copulation may begin almost immediately, or it may take several hours to occur. The pair may copulate only once, or they may copulate several times over many days. It is usually wise to house the pair together for several days (if they are not permanent cage mates), to allow for multiple copulations, thereby helping to ensure good fertility.

Care of the Gravid Female

With some luck, the female will become gravid (pregnant) shortly after the animals have bred. Isolate the female once she begins displaying such symptoms. This will help keep her stress level low and allow you to provide better care for her.

Provide gravid females with a suitable egg-deposition chamber. A plastic storage container or cat litter pan makes a suitable chamber. Experienced breeders often transfer females to egg chambers outside of their cages shortly before oviposition occurs, but this only introduces unnecessary complexity to the process that novices are wise to avoid – just place the container inside the female's enclosure and let her find it.

Fill the chamber about two-thirds full with slightly damp soil and pack it gently into place. The soil must not be wet, but it must have enough moisture to allow the lizard to create a stable tunnel and egg chamber. As a rule of thumb, you should be able to compress the soil into a clump when you squeeze it in your hand, without causing any water to trickle out.

Near the end of the gestation, which typically lasts about three to four weeks, females develop very plump abdomens. In some cases, the faint outline of eggs can be seen through the abdominal wall.

Do not handle gravid females unless absolutely necessary, and try to keep their stress level as low as possible.

Egg Deposition

If the female finds the egg chamber satisfactory, she will crawl into the container and dig a small tunnel that ends in an enlarged chamber. She will then turn around and deposit 10 to 30 eggs (usually around 20). After she has completed the process, she will climb back out of the tunnel and cover it completely.

It is a good idea to mist her thoroughly at this time, so she can rehydrate. Misting her will also help to rinse the dirt off her.

If the female does not find the egg chamber to her liking, she may dig multiple tunnels or simply crawl back out of the egg chamber without depositing her eggs. This can be problematic, as retained eggs represent a very serious health problem.

Try to adjust the substrate in the egg chamber with hopes that she will try again and find your changes helpful. You may need to add water to the substrate or dry out the substrate by mixing in fresh, dry soil.

Always observe gravid dragons carefully for signs that suggest they are unable to deposit their eggs. For example, egg-bound females may pace back and forth in the cage, dig multiple burrows without depositing eggs or simply become lethargic. If your female displays these signs, or she does not deposit the eggs by day 45 of the gestation process, you must take her to your veterinarian without delay.

Egg binding is a serious medical condition that can become fatal very quickly. However, with prompt attention, your vet may be able to administer medications which will help her deposit eggs. If that fails to have the desired effect, your vet may perform surgery on the female, to remove the eggs from her body. Such eggs are highly unlikely to hatch, but this will usually save the life of your female. However, she may be rendered unable to breed by such operations.

Retrieving the Eggs

Once the female has deposited her eggs and you have ensured she is rehydrated and in good health, begin excavating the tunnel. Use a gentle touch and take care not to damage the eggs.

Avoid rotating the eggs while removing and transferring them to the egg chamber. It is often helpful to mark the top of each egg with a graphite pencil. This way, you can be sure to place them in the same orientation in which they settled into the egg mass.

Separate any eggs that come apart easily, but never use excessive force when doing so. If a cluster of eggs will not separate easily, they should be left attached to each other and incubated as they are.

Place the eggs in a deli cup or plastic food container, half-filled with slightly dampened vermiculite (most keepers use a 1:1 ratio of vermiculite to water, by weight). When in doubt, subject the vermiculite to the same test used for the egg deposition substrate – it should clump when compressed, but not release any water.

Bury the eggs halfway into the vermiculite and close the container. Try to space the eggs so that none are in direct contact with any others.

Egg Incubation

Bearded dragon eggs are fairly easy to incubate. You can purchase a commercially produced incubator or construct your own. Most any incubator designed for use with reptile eggs will suffice, but it is wise to test the unit and ensure it holds consistent temperatures before you are faced with eggs.

You can make your own incubator by filling a 10-gallon aquarium with a few inches of water. Place an aquarium heater in the water, and set the thermostat at the desired temperature. Place a brick in the water and rest the egg chamber on top of the brick. Cover the aquarium with a glass top to keep the heat and moisture contained.

Set your incubator to about 84 degrees Fahrenheit (29 degrees Celsius) for the duration of the incubation time. At this temperature, most of the young will hatch in about 60 days. However, some clutches take more or less time than this, and incubation may range from 50 to 75 days.

Individual eggs may progress at slightly different rates, so hatchlings may emerge from the clutch over the course of a period of several days. Many of the hatchlings will remain in their egg for 24 hours or so, while they absorb the remainder of their egg yolk. Do not attempt to remove the lizards from their eggs – allow them to exit on their own.

Neonatal Husbandry

Once the young begin hatching from their eggs, you can remove them from the egg box and place them in a small cage or "nursery." Do not attempt to remove any hatchlings from their eggs. If any of the young emerge with their yolk sacs still attached, leave them in the egg box until they have absorbed the yolk.

A 20-gallon aquarium with a bare floor and a screened lid makes a satisfactory nursery. Place several small branches in the tank and add plenty of plant clippings to provide the young with some form of cover.

Mist the young several times per day and keep the temperatures at about 80 degrees Fahrenheit (27 degrees Celsius). You can initiate feeding trials within a day or two, but do not be surprised if the young lizards do not begin eating for several days.

Keep the young in the nursery until they begin feeding regularly. At this point, you can begin breaking them into small groups and placing them in screened enclosures.

Hatchling bearded dragons have slightly different body proportions than adults do.

Further Reading

Never stop learning more about your new pet's natural history, biology and captive care. This is the only way to ensure that you are providing him or her with the highest quality of life possible.

Books

Bookstores and online book retailers offer a treasure trove of information that will advance your quest for knowledge. Your local library may also carry some books about bearded dragons, which you can borrow for no charge.

University libraries are a great place for finding old, obscure or academically oriented books about bearded dragons.

Herpetology: An Introductory Biology of Amphibians and Reptiles
Laurie J. Vitt, Janalee P. Caldwell
Academic Press, 2013

Understanding Reptile Parasites: A Basic Manual for Herpetoculturists & Veterinarians
Roger Klingenberg D.V.M.
Advanced Vivarium Systems, 1997

Infectious Diseases and Pathology of Reptiles: Color Atlas and Text
Elliott Jacobson
CRC Press

Designer Reptiles and Amphibians
Richard D. Bartlett, Patricia Bartlett
Barron's Educational Series

Lizards: Windows to the Evolution of Diversity
Eric R. Pianka, Laurie J. Vit
University of California Press

The Bearded Dragon Manual
Philippe De Vosjoli
BowTie Incorporated

Bearded Dragons
Richard D. Bartlett, Patricia Bartlett

Barron's Educational Series

Bearded Dragon
Tom Mazorlig
Tfh Publications Incorporated

Magazines

Because magazines are typically published monthly or bi-monthly, they occasionally offer more up-to-date information than books do. Magazine articles are obviously not as comprehensive as books typically are, but they still have considerable value.

Reptiles Magazine
www.reptilesmagazine.com/
Covering reptiles commonly kept in captivity.

Practical Reptile Keeping
http://www.practicalreptilekeeping.co.uk/
Practical Reptile Keeping is a popular publication aimed at beginning and advanced hobbies. Topics include the care and maintenance of popular reptiles as well as information on wild reptiles.

Websites

The internet has made it much easier to find information about reptiles than it has ever been. However, you must use discretion when deciding which websites to trust.

While knowledgeable breeders, keepers and academics operate some websites, many who maintain reptile-oriented websites lack the same dedication and scientific rigor. Anyone with a computer and internet connection can launch a website and say virtually anything they want. Always consider the source of the information before making any husbandry decisions.

The Reptile Report
www.thereptilereport.com/
The Reptile Report is a news-aggregating website that accumulates interesting stories and features about reptiles from around the world.

Kingsnake.com
www.kingsnake.com

After starting as a small website for gray-banded kingsnake enthusiasts, Kingsnake.com has become one of the largest reptile-oriented portals in the hobby. The site features classified advertisements, a breeder directory, message forums and other resources.

The Vivarium and Aquarium News
www.vivariumnews.com/
The online version of the former print publication, The Vivarium and Aquarium News provides in-depth coverage of different reptiles and amphibians in both captive and wild contexts.

Journals

Journals are the primary place professional scientists turn when they need to learn about dragons. While they may not make light reading, hobbyists stand to learn a great deal from journals.

Herpetologica
www.hljournals.org/
Published by The Herpetologists' League, Herpetologica, and its companion publication, Herpetological Monographs cover all aspects of reptile and amphibian research.

Journal of Herpetology
www.ssarherps.org/
Produced by the Society for the Study of Reptiles and Amphibians, the Journal of Herpetology is a peer-reviewed publication covering a variety of reptile-related topics.

Copeia
www.asihcopeiaonline.org/
Copeia is published by the American Society of Ichthyologists and Herpetologists. A peer-reviewed journal, Copeia covers all aspects of the biology of reptiles, amphibians and fish.

Nature
www.nature.com/
Although Nature covers all aspects of the natural world, many issues contain information that lizard enthusiasts are sure to find interesting.

Supplies

You can obtain most of what you need to maintain bearded dragons through your local pet store, but online retailers offer another option.

Big Apple Pet Supply
http://www.bigappleherp.com
Big Apple Pet Supply carries most common husbandry equipment, including heating devices, water dishes and substrates.

LLLReptile
http://www.lllreptile.com
LLL Reptile carries a wide variety of husbandry tools, heating devices, lighting products and more.

Doctors Foster and Smith
http://www.drsfostersmith.com
Foster and Smith is a veterinarian-owned retailer that supplies husbandry-related items to pet keepers.

Support Organizations

Sometimes, the best way to learn about bearded dragons is to reach out to other keepers and breeders. Check out these organizations, and search for others in your geographic area.

The National Reptile & Amphibian Advisory Council
http://www.nraac.org/
The National Reptile & Amphibian Advisory Council seeks to educate the hobbyists, legislators and the public about reptile and amphibian related issues.

American Veterinary Medical Association
www.avma.org
The AVMA is a good place for Americans to turn if you are having trouble finding a suitable reptile veterinarian.

The World Veterinary Association
http://www.worldvet.org/
The World Veterinary Association is a good resource for finding suitable reptile veterinarians worldwide.

References

Anderson, S. P. (2003). The Phylogenetic Definition of Reptilia. *Systematic Biology*.

C. J. Raxworthy, M. R. (2002). Chameleon radiation by oceanic dispersal. *Letters to Nature*.

Djordje Grbic, e. a. (2015). Phylogeography and support vector machine classification of colour variation in panther chameleons. *Molecular Ecology*.

Gary W. Ferguson, W. G. (2002). Effects of Artificial Ultraviolet Light Exposure on Reproductive Success of the Female Panther Chameleon (Furcifer pardalis) in Captivity. *Zoo Biology*.

Leeuwen, D. G. (2015). The Diet of Free-Roaming Australian Central Bearded Dragons (Pogona vitticeps). *Zoo Biology*.

Müller. (2014). Zur möglichen Lebenserwartung von Bartagamen (Pogona vitticeps). *Reptilia* .

SCHULTE, J. M. (2001). Correlates of active body temperatures and microhabitat occupation in nine species of central Australian agamid lizards. *Austral Ecology*.

William E Cooper, J. (2000). Chemosensory discrimination of plant and animal foods by the omnivorous iguanian lizard Pogona vitticeps. *Canadian Journal of Zoology*.

Index

CPSIA information can be obtained
at www.ICGtesting.com
Printed in the USA
BVHW092300231120
593995BV00004B/192

9 781911 142539